T. M. Wainwright.
36 Cambridge Rd.
Clacton On Sea.
Essex.

GH00454975

WORKING WITH HORSES

REX HAMEY

BATSFORD ACADEMIC and EDUCATIONAL LTD   London

Typeset by Granada Graphics
and printed in Great Britain by
The Pitman Press Ltd
Bath, Somerset
for the publishers
Batsford Academic and Educational Limited
an imprint of B T Batsford Limited
4 Fitzhardinge Street, London W1H 0AH

ISBN 0 7134 4461 4

Contents

Acknowledgment

For their time and the facilities freely given to help guide young horse lovers into gainful employment I would like to thank the following:

J Onions, staff and students at West Oxfordshire Technical College; T F Williams of Hereford Technical College; A H B Hart, T M Delaney, Christine Stafford, Anthony Wakeham, Secretaries of MFHA, NAG, SLA and BETA; Cotswold Hunt Kennels, Andoversford; R Hartop, Shipton Oliffe, Cheltenham; Stan and Elaine Mellor, Lambourne; Mrs G Pink, Badgeworth Riding Centre, Cheltenham; and R Stokes, Sturt Farm, Burford.

Captions to photographs between pages 76 and 77

Taking the horses out for a lunge

Young riders practising a small jump together

Lungeing a horse over poles

Long reining a young horse

Leading round yearlings at Newmarket sales

Leading out mares with their foals
Reproduced by courtesy of Laurie Morton Photography, Newmarket

An early morning gallop

Horses of the Kings Troop being taught to accept the noise of a brassband
Reproduced by courtesy of the London District Horse Guards

Mounted policewoman on duty in Hyde Park
Reproduced by courtesy of the Commissioner of Police of the Metropolis

Putting on a stable bandage

A farrier's apprentice learns to shape a special shoe
Reproduced by courtesy of Laurie Morton Photography, Newmarket

Cleaning the saddles in the tack room. Saddle horses are used to support the saddles

Giving an intravenous injection

Picking out a hoof after cub-hunting

Mucking out the stable using a skip for the dung and a wheelbarrow for the soiled straw

Author with one of his stallions

Photographs by Rex Hamey unless otherwise stated
Diagrams by Lizzie Hamey

Introduction

Horses are part of our national heritage and British trained grooms are to be found all round the world.

Racing alone provides ten thousand people with jobs breeding the horses and then training them. Another ninety thousand are employed in work which relies on racing, such as transport, race-course administration and stewarding, catering, journalism, secretarial jobs and the betting offices.

Two million adults are estimated to ride every year, and when you add to this the number of children riding ponies this figure is probably doubled. Combining all the work involved with the care of horses and ponies, their food, and maintaining tack and all the equipment associated with the stables, as well as the work involved in designing and making of clothes for the riders whether jodphurs, jackets and hats for the informal ride, or the formal habits for the hunt or show jumping events, these jobs together with those of racing, show the horse industry to be a huge source of employment and commerce.

It is no longer sufficient just to be dedicated to horses to enable you to get a job working with them. If you go into stables or a stud to work, you must be prepared to study and practise the skills needed to gain the respect of your supervisors; you must be ready to take advantage of responsibilities that maybe offered to you because the opportunity to progress in the horse world will depend on the success you make of these chances.

Any future employers will want proof of your ability, and having the qualifications helps to ensure promotion and the better wages that go with it. Proper training should also make the job easier and improve the welfare of the horses in your care.

Working with horses to earn a living may be your dream but before trying to turn that dream into reality, I suggest you read this book carefully, for in it I have explained thoroughly all the different types of jobs actually with the horses and other work that brings you into contact with them. Any work with animals, other than pets, is termed 'labour intensive'. This means it entails long hours of work spread over all the week, including Saturday and Sunday, all of the year, in all kinds of weather, and sometimes it is physically exhausting.

Television programmes show you only the glamorous side of working with horses, and going to a race-meeting, spending a day at the local horse show or even having several lessons at a riding school cannot give you a clear understanding of all the time and work that is necessary to prepare the horses to take part in the competitive events.

The first few months of full-time working in a stable or stud will probably be tiring and demanding on you. It may be very difficult to keep up some of your other activities and pleasures, simply because you do not have the energy or time for them. Working with horses tends to alter your interests and your outlook on life.

Most of the people who are successful and stay with horses all their lives, usually make their decision during their schooldays. You may already have experience of teachers who get annoyed with you if you have a passionate and distracting interest in horses and ponies which they say affects your school work, especially when you should be studying hard for your CSE or O level examinations.

I believe the education system should help such genuinely motivated children who wish to work in any of the labour intensive jobs, not only those concerned with animals and leisure. But at the same time the children themselves should study and get qualifications in those subjects which can benefit them in their chosen careers.

My life with horses

The summer after my father had ridden the winner of the Grand National steeplechase, my elder brother and I were taken to the local railway station, with a hand cart, to collect a crate containing two young Shetland ponies. I was nearly three years old at that time and ponies and horses have been in my life ever since.

Playing, in those early school days of mine, was usually with the ponies. Most of my friends had ponies too and I cannot remember actually learning to ride. As my father had started to train race-horses as well as being a jockey, my brother and I were expected to be good riders. Many of the wealthy people brought their children's ponies to us when their own children were not riding them often enough to keep them well behaved.

Riding some of these ponies was difficult and my father liked to be near when we did so. To supervise our riding he allowed the ponies to be exercised behind the string of racehorses. Just after my seventh birthday, when I had no pony to ride, he put me on a quiet old hurdler to trot round the roads. Later, being trusted to exercise a racehorse every morning before going to school increased my desire to be a jockey and soon I regarded ponies as playthings. The start of the war, which stopped racing for a while and took my father into the Army, soon altered my ideas because there were no horses to ride. Our home and stables were taken over to house part of a firm evacuated from the south coast and, in a rush my mother took us to live at her father's farm. There were only cart-horses there and helping with those to do the farmwork was very tame. However, a neighbouring horse dealer came to my rescue by giving me pocket money to break-in ponies, which he bought in batches in Wales, and these were very wild.

Petrol rationing created a huge demand for the ponies which could be used for both riding and driving in the country areas, so there were plenty of thrills in the haste to get them ready for sale. The busy life of the farm and working with the ponies did not give me much time to think about my ambition to be a jockey, so at the age of fifteen it gave me a bit of a shock when my mother asked an old friend of my father if he would take me as an apprentice jockey. He refused because I was over nine stone in weight and he did not think I could make racing a career. My mother therefore made me stay at school and I studied with the prospect of becoming an architect. But gradually competitive field games claimed more of my interest and when my father returned from the Army to start training horses again, I naturally wanted to help and I rode every morning, then hurried home to groom some of the horses in the evening.

Luckily I had not put on more than a few pounds in weight and my parents allowed me to leave the technical college to work in the stables for a year before I went into the Army at eighteen, for the then compulsory National Service.

Working in the racing stables awakened my dream to be a jockey. Perhaps it was fortunate for me that my father had a struggle to get going as a trainer again, for other people brought to him hunters and show-jumpers to be broken-in and schooled. Most of this extra riding occupied my afternoons when the stable lads had their traditional rest. The opportunity to practise different styles of riding improved my ability and prompted a few of the owners, who also had racehorses, to let me ride some of their horses in races, just before I went into the Army.

The regiment I joined had twenty horses for recreation and my job was to train some for competition, either show-jumping or racing. Fate was again good to me for a month after I arrived in Germany the world famous Colonel Paul Rodzianko, who had trained the Irish Olympic team and studied under Caprilli, accepted twelve horsemen from the whole of the British Army of the Rhine, to train as riding instructors, and I was one of the three to pass the course. As soon as I could I left the Army and dedicated myself to becoming a jockey. To keep my weight down to be able to ride the lightly weighted handicapped horses in my father's stables meant donning several sweaters and running about five miles twice a week. This effort made me very fit and I was noticed by Frenchie Nicholson and John Roberts, two of the other trainers in the village, with the result that they gave me mounts on some of their runners. Winners brought more offers, and the following year I took a retainer to ride for Ivor Anthony, who had trained the famous Brown Jack. Besides riding for other people, I kept this association for seven years until the stable moved to Kingsclere, unfortunately the gallops (on Watership Down) were not able to stand winter use and steeplechasers could not be trained there. Bob Turnell had some of the horses, which I continued to ride in races, but not enough to pay me a retainer as jockey, and Colonel Whitbread and Jock Witney took first claim on my services for a year, then Fred Rimell asked me to ride for his stable. The injuries I had been getting had given me more time to broaden my interest in training horses and other aspects of the horse business, including breeding and the people working with horses.

Jack Yeomans, my father-in-law, was impressed by my study of the training and managing of a complete horse enterprise and suggested I started such a venture on his farm. Buying the right sort of horses cheaply and finding some boys to teach my methods of exercising horse and riders to make racehorses and jockeys, paid off for we had several big winners at Liverpool, Sandown and many other courses while I was riding the horses. Ken White, David Cartwright, Dennis Atkins and Peter Warner went on to become well known as steeplechase jockeys after I left. Willie Stephenson had seen the success I was having with limited money and offered me the chance, with more scope, to do the same for him. There were over a hundred horses in training at Royston and a stud had just been started. Besides training the Derby and Grand National winners, Willie Stephenson had headed both Flat and Jumping trainers lists. My job allowed me to continue to ride in races, assist him training his string and have some more at Tudor Stud, where I was a manager with my own staff. The breeding stud was only one stallion and about twenty mares when I took over, but within four years I expanded it to house four stallions and a hundred and forty visiting mares each season.

In addition to breaking in the thirty yearling racehorses annually, about sixty horses came to board at the stud while they were waiting to be shipped to different parts of the world. This business brought many visitors from abroad and I encouraged students to stay long enough to learn about horse management. Having both foreign and British students, as well as advising owners of valuable horses, meant keeping up to date with my study of veterinary practice and trading regulations.

As I was able to take some of these horses abroad to such places as Cyprus, France, Germany, Hong Kong, Ireland, Italy, Japan, Morocco, Norway and Singapore, I was able to see stable management in different climates round the globe; and with Mr Robert Crowhurst and Mr Peter Rossdale as veterinaries visiting the stud each week for several years, my knowledge improved enormously.

While my professional career was with thoroughbreds for racing, many of my friends and social activities were somehow connected to other sports and uses of horses. For example, an invitation from the Queen Mother to ride in a jockeys' invitation show jumping competition at Richmond, began a whole series of these events as other shows followed suit. I expect you have noticed a few that have been televised lately. The show jumping people lend the horses and obviously like the riders to have some practise, under their guidance, to help them to do well in the ring and avoid upsetting their horses.

Hunting young steeplechasers has always been a very good introduction to get them used to crowds and jumping. From the pony club days, a day out with the hounds, teaching a young animal how to carry its rider across the countryside, has given me much pleasure. Probably the satisfaction of seeing horses and riders which I have schooled being successful, has helped me increase my own desire to teach young people entering the horse industry. Starting a small New Forest pony stud as a sideline, and writing about the finances and conditions of employment of the horse industry also have had considerable influence on my desire to teach.

Showing the ponies in their classes and selling them afterwards brought contacts with riding schools and people buying ponies (often for the first time) to enjoy the outdoor horsey sports. This also meant giving advice on the care of the animals at their homes, and guiding the children who became so keen on riding that they were determined to work with horses after leaving school.

While I was seeking information to include in my articles for the press on all the business and employment dependent on horses, I met John Onions of the West Oxfordshire Technical College, who invited me to put my experience to good use by helping to teach the students on their horse husbandry course. The questions asked by the students, who come from all over Britain and a few from overseas, and who have already worked with horses for a short time, prompted me to write a book based on my years in the horse industry to supply the answers they need to complete their knowledge. This in turn lead to being asked to write this book as a guide to the many school leavers thinking of trying to earn their living working with horses.

Hard work has been necessary for me to take advantage of the chances that came my way, even with the good start given to me by my father. I wonder if I would still be thinking that I could have ridden a Grand National winner like him if I had carried on with studying to be an architect and not pushed myself to be a jockey.

Whether you are lucky enough to start your life with horses in a similar manner does not matter. The reason I have written this book is to tell you the branch of the industry you will be able to make the most of your talent and physique, and hopefully you will make similar efforts to succeed.

Horses as a means of employment

The horse industry

To call the population of horses and the people who earn their livelihood with them an industry may seem strange but, from early civilization to the present day, horses have been helping man by providing a means of transport and power. Today we think of them as animals used for sport and leisure, as in a very few instances horses are still working as they did before the engine was invented.

It is difficult to state the actual size of the horse industry. The number of horses in Britain is only estimated and the variations of between one-and-a-half-million down to three-quarters-of-a-million depend on the source of the information. Similarly the exact number of people who make their living in the industry is largely guess work, although fairly accurate figures are available in the highly commercial and professional sports.

Racing and breeding thoroughbreds is responsible for a massive annual turnover of £2,500 million from betting alone. To support the racing on the sixty racecourses requires an administrative staff of about two thousand people. The twelve thousand racehorses are owned by nearly thirteen thousand individuals and companies distributed among eight hundred trainers who, in turn, employ four thousand stable staff and seven hundred jockeys. Breeding to supply the demand for the two and three year old horses which run in the majority of the flat races, gives an income to the owners of six thousand studs where another five thousand workers are in full- or part-time employment.

The professional show jumpers and horse trial riders are a relatively new innovation in their respective sports, but the published prices of the few famous horses to be sold, indicate the rapid growth of the sports as a commercial venture. Sponsorship from advertising using the horses and the large increase in television showing have boosted the chance of making a living out of these sports for several hundred equestrians.

The Riding Schools Association claim to have fourteen hundred approved establishments as members, in addition it is estimated two thousand more are in business to give riding lessons, and possibly another three thousand stables pay their expenses by hiring out and dealing in horses for the occasional riders.

Hunting, polo, and the many people who keep horses for pleasure, swell the numbers at an increasing rate, the Riding Club movement has spread rapidly throughout Britain, so much so that riding is now officially recognised as a 'growth sport' with about four hundred clubs in all parts of the country.

The grooms and workers in the industry

Most of the horses taking part in the competitive events and the strenuous equestrian sports are stabled and need grooms to feed and clean them. This is because most of their owners earn the money to keep them from other businesses and professions. However, because the horses are usually in privately owned stables and studs with only a single groom or a few grooms or workers employed in each place, there is difficulty in the forming of any trade union. The individuality of the owners and employers similarly oppose efforts to band the grooms into organisations. Some sports and breed societies make joining and paying subscriptions a condition of taking part in the events under their control. Racing and show jumping have systems of licensing and registration for horses and people actively engaged in them. The lack of these unions does not stop the thousands of employees in the industry from making a reasonable living and having a happy life in it.

Opportunities

The chance of fame and fortune are similar to those of the stage and other jobs to which dedication, lengthy training and hard work are necessary, combined with luck and the ability to make the most of any opportunities that come your way.

Everyday living expenses should be covered by normal wages, but these will not allow luxuries. Careful planning of your career to gain experience must also be aimed at learning a bit more about the horses and improving your skills to be better than the other grooms. It is surprising how a little extra effort can earn the added respect of your employer, and this is the first step to the top of your branch of the horse world. With dedication and skill there are few barriers.

Horses as a means of employment

I would stress that there is no lasting short cut to the top. Money paid by people trying to buy fame through expensive horses trained by professionals is usually short lived. Hard work and devotion pay dividends and the chance to ride in a competition or race is a prize to be won. That extra effort previously put in will often tilt the balance when there is equal ability between the rival riders for the mount.

The opportunities to make headway in your career differ greatly in the various types of work and sports involving horses. The chances of competing on the polo field, at a horse-trial, riding in a point-to-point, or jumping a horse in the show ring are slim. These are mainly amateur rider sports and the people riding the horses pay handsomely for the privilege. However, most of them earn their living in a different profession which means that they have to pay grooms to exercise and look after the horses. Gaining experience and being paid at the same time is sensible. Later, when you have gathered enough skill and knowledge to train horses for one of these sports, preparing them for clients and selling can make good profits.

Riding

Because of the immaturity of flat racehorses, light weight riders are a necessity in the training stables and to find adults small enough to exercise the horses is difficult. Consequently many young boys enter the racing yards in the hope of becoming jockeys. Few make the grade but once they have learnt the job thoroughly, they find many opportunities to earn a living among the horses; some eventually become head lads and stud grooms. In fact nearly all the flat race jockeys started their careers in this way and a good many trainers have similar beginnings.

Girls being naturally lighter than boys are finding it easier to get work as grooms in the racing stables. Trainers have also found that their more sympathetic nature suits some of the highly strung and nervous thoroughbreds.

Nearly all jobs where riding exercise on the horses is part of the work, people over twelve stone will not be employed. Being heavy does not bar you from working with horses for there are many places and chances for you on the studs and the mixed yards where strength for handling young and difficult horses is needed.

A division between racing and the British Horse Society

The tradition of the Racing and Thoroughbred breeding industry began over two hundred years ago. This has evolved into the present system where personal recommendation and service received are still uppermost. Learning skill and gaining knowledge are judged to take time under the professional guidance of a master of a stud or stable. The British Horse Society which is currently rearranging its examination and training schemes, started in the early sixties to try and bring some order into the widely spread and varying standards of the rapidly growing private or amateur sector of the horse industry in Britain. Before that the Pony Club movement and the Institute of The Horse, liaising with the Army, helped with training and instructing any part of the relatively small numbers of equestrians that it was in the national interest to improve. Most of the riding then was restricted to wealthy people able to afford horses and grooms. Hunting, polo and hacking for exercise was not enjoyed by the ordinary working class. Somehow the two sides of the industry, or rather their authorities, have failed to design the qualifications and examination system which gives the same value to the whole of the British horse industry, so if you study to gain British Horse Society certificates and want to cross over into the racing side, it is likely your new employer will make you start at the bottom until you prove your worth. It is more difficult going the other way, for regulations bar promotion without the necessary certificates to show.

Very little can be done to alter this unfortunate state of affairs. My advice is to remember it and avoid being inconvenienced. The basic training of grooms and indeed most of the subsequent schooling and treatment of horses and their management is too similar to be divided.

Employers

Many people keep horses purely for their own pleasure. Sometimes the true costs are more than they can afford and, through a mistaken idea of keeping up their own image in the community, believe that while the horses must have the best of everything, their employees should make do with the bare necessities of living, and so pay very

21

low wages. The truth soon becomes widely known by the grooms passing on information about the financial state and the owner's struggle to keep the horses and stable going, and such places often close or are reduced in size.

The successful stables and studs, on the other hand, achieve long lasting service and loyalty from their paid staff and customers, much envied and respected by everyone in the industry. It is therefore difficult to find a vacancy for work in the better places. But if you can wait or are able to apply at least six months ahead, the training you will receive and just having had experience at such a place, can help you to secure other jobs and promotion during the next few years of your career. Seldom can a trainee have a chance of rising to a position of responsibility unless he is prepared to stay with one employer for several years.

Between the two extremes come the majority of studs and stables, owned by hard working people, dependent on horses for pleasure and business. Their success or failure will be affected by the staff they employ, because horses seem to improve with good handling and regress when grooms are not putting much effort into their work.

The yards from which happy voices are heard, with the horses jumping and kicking in exuberance at the start of their daily exercise, will be the ones having the winners. The losers by those vital inches, seconds or faults, will come from the dull and morose places, where, as is usually the case, the boss is a grumbler and in turn the staff are miserable.

How you can judge a place to work

Although it may be advisable to take the first job with horses you are offered, because all experience and training received while you are actually working with horses will help your career, it is important for you to be able to plan out the steps which will enable you to get a good training before you start in your quest to make working with horses a worthwhile and possibly lifetime career.

To help you understand the differences in the types of work in the studs and stables, each one is dealt with later, but here I wish to give you an idea which is easy to apply to all future places where you would like to work. Try to think of yourself as a prospective customer going to conduct some business at the stud or stable. When you arrive it is doubtful, until you tell someone the reason for your visit, that the staff know why you are there. The clean, tidy establishments with sleek good-tempered horses, attended by an efficient cheerful staff who make you feel welcome to see and hear about the animals in their care, is more likely to be a job that lasts and provides good training than the sloppy, unkempt stable yard with the workers dodging round corners out of your way. And do not be mislead by brand new freshly painted stables with dropped empty cigarette packets and slovenly cleaning up in the yard which you will notice while you are waiting for someone to see you. Another point to watch is the dress of the grooms. Good grooms are usually clean and tidy. In other words, if you cannot look after yourself, how can you possibly keep horses clean and tidy? A glance at the head person and the other grooms will quickly show you the standards set.

Preparing yourself

Starting work with horses

Every person who earns a living by working or dealing with horses had to be taught the correct way to handle a horse, or how to ride properly and the best method of grooming. Although trial and error may enable you to find a way to clean a pony and get it to carry you about – possibly well enough to win at the local gymkhana – once you decide to make your living by working with horses you must learn the accepted methods. Some of you already have ponies and or may have parents with horses, so you can start to practise at the Pony Club or under a qualified instructor. The motivation to seek employment in a stable or a stud is usually because of an instinctive love of horses and does not necessarily follow definite family habit. While that early start may give you an advantage in the very beginning, once training and working really get under way, it is dedication and your ability to do your share that count with an employer.

During the time you are working with horses you will find many people who entered by chance, that is to say they were offered a job and took it because of their enjoyment of horses. Often these people have not had a sound training and possess no qualifications. Gradually employers are realising the importance of giving the young entrants into the studs and stables the training to make them efficient and responsible. To train a horse requires repeating exercises over and over again. Having to do this with horses seems to give experienced horse people a similar tolerance when they are training young persons. However you will be expected to keep to time, be respectful and reasonably clean in your dress and show your enthusiasm does not falter by learning the easy tasks fairly quickly. The horses and their well being are the first considerations of responsible horse managers, so if you upset the horses or the smooth running of the stable routine do not be surprised to receive the rough side of the boss's tongue. Most horsemen and women have quick reactions and swear volubly in defence of the animals in their charge.

Will I be able to do the work?

The work in stables has evolved by several hundred years of tradition to include a regular intake of school leavers. Until recent years these were only fourteen years of age, now you have to be two years older so you should be able to cope better, for the initial tasks are still the same. The riding, if you are engaged to exercise the horses, will be under supervision until you are capable and judged responsible enough to be allowed to ride by yourself. The weight you are has some importance in the type of work that you may choose. Boys over seven stone at sixteen and girls over eight stone at seventeen will find it hard to get into flat racing stables. Another stone at those ages is about the limit in the National Hunt steeplechasing yards. Generally employers like riders to be under eleven stone when fully grown. Being grossly overweight in relation to your height makes riding difficult so unless you can convince an employer of your ability, overweight is a handicap. Obviously anyone with serious physical defects such as brittle bones, epileptic fits of a re-occurring nature, haemophilia and very violent tempers will have little chance of finding an employer willing to take him on. Parents in these cases have a moral duty to prevent their children getting hurt, and allowing them to seek this work in the first place is wrong.

Sometimes the size of hunters, thoroughbreds or shire horses can be frightening and fear of getting hurt may cause you great anxiety in the first few months of being left in a stable to work with a horse by yourself. Horses are timid creatures by nature, but confidence and affinity to work with them should be tried and tested by going to a place where you can handle ponies to start with. Gradually you become accustomed to the way they react to humans. You build your own confidence if you start with ponies to match your size, and you can progress to horses by degrees. The shock of being put in a stable with an unknown large beast or sitting five feet above the ground on a bundle of living muscle used to frighten many of the fourteen year old apprentices going into racing, so much so that it was often years before they learnt to ride, even if they had the courage to stay at the training stable.

Preparing yourself

Some hints to help you find work before you leave school

Training people for work from the very beginning in any job is expensive. When it is with animals the job does not always have a profit margin and is sometimes dependent on the enjoyment the employer gets from keeping the stables and staff (which means the whole of the expenses of running their establishment comes out of their own pocket) it is only more economical to take trainees if the trainees have some experience before they leave school and are paid for learning while working. Today, showing some determination and proof of making an effort to prepare yourself for your selected career counts as much in the horse world as in any other walk of life, therefore begin as soon as possible.

The expense of keeping ponies and horses puts that beyond the means of most people who are satisfied to spend their working life looking after horses belonging to other people. Although present-day costs are making hundreds of true enthusiastic equestrians work for pay in an employer's yard in order to be able to afford the keep of their own horse.

Paying for riding lessons or riding holidays is also expensive and does not really supply the experience of handling and working with ponies or horses that you need to embark on a long and fulfilling life with them.

If your parents can afford it while you are at school, some lucky ones among you may have your own ponies or be able to ride a friend's pony, but you will still need lessons. The riding schools are the best places to start because their animals are selected for that purpose, and usually the enclosed area or barn gives the learner confidence to be able to progress in the art of horsemanship. Seldom is a horse-loving child too far away from some sort of stable in Britain now that it is impossible for him to get there regularly. Some of you may be lucky enough to be within a few minutes walk, others may find the most they can manage is one day a fortnight. Even in the big cities there are still horses to be found, and if you are determined, you can find their stables and means of getting there. The object in finding these nearby stables while you are in your last year or eighteen months at school, is for you to start getting some actual 'work experience' in stables and with horses, because in spite of the claims by employers to treat all school leavers and recruits into their stables or stud on an equal merit and train them up to the standard they require, it is increasingly doubtful if an applicant without some knowledge and proof of having been doing some stable tasks, such as tack cleaning, mucking out and occasionally grooming dirty or sweaty horses will get very far in his quest for work. Admittedly riding is an asset to finding a job, many girls able to ride well enough for competition are taking jobs straight away after leaving school, but on the basis of a working pupil for a year or more. Therefore it is essential to prove your worth by a regular spare time job, even if you do it without pay, although most places will offer free rides, outings or reimbursement of bus fares.

Insurance

Accidents do happen, especially when both children and horses are involved. So make sure the person allowing you to gain experience in their stables has insurance covering your part-time work. Taking silly risks can result in serious injury, but nevertheless some things that working with horses entails, demands a bit of courage. Accepting this challenge is very different from not seeing danger. Wait until your bravery is rewarded by full-time pay, or you are at your place with your own horses.

The importance of education

Qualifications are becoming almost essential to getting promotion and the increases in wages and opportunities which you will want during your life. Studying the right subjects and passing the necessary CSE or O levels while you are at school can open the way to further education later on. Nine of the agricultural and technical colleges with courses in horse husbandry have a minimum education standard for entry (see the following chapter on Training and Education). Biology and agricultural sciences are naturally subjects to choose, as well as English and Mathematics which would seem to provide you with the most satisfying career chances and which may be of future use depending on the branch of the industry and your natural skill; other choices could be metalwork, accountancy and typing. Your careers officer and your parents can usually help if you decide in good time to start the study aimed at passing the examinations, but do try to plan ahead.

Certificates and references

Before you leave school, those of you lucky enough to have belonged to the Pony Club or to take the CSE mode three examination in horse riding and stable work — now available in some parts of the country — should already have some certificates of your ability to handle horses or ponies. References from your school teachers and the people for whom you have worked with horses, or in other jobs, are always a good thing to present to your prospective employer as they show real proof of your intent to work and usually contain something nice about your character as well.

Obtain and keep safe and clean these certificates and references when you have earned the right to ask the person to give you one. Leaving school or finishing the job may lose your contact with the teacher or employer, then when you go for some important interview you will be unable to produce them. People today can choose from the number of applicants who present all their details together and are loath to wait while someone is searching for theirs.

Most people in the horse industry have a wide circle of friends and acquaintances in the industry, so personal recommendation from one of these people can be a big asset when seeking work, but permission must be asked and they must give it before you pass their name to be contacted by a prospective employer. It is also a good idea to collect the names, addresses and telephone numbers of your own personal contacts in the horse world who may be able to give you some recommendation should the need arise. Again good manners and common sense decree a polite request for their permission to be approached should the necessity arise.

Job seeking

Making an application to an employer is an art today irrespective of your age or ability. Being successful and getting the position of employment is the only result that is satisfactory. Nothing is more likely to make you feel despondent than waiting, knowing many other people have replied to the advertisement for the job for which you are suited and have written.

In general, the replies to advertisements for the vacant jobs in stables or studs are several score to each one. While it would be nice to have the advertiser reply to every applicant, this is seldom the case and although most are read by someone, the boss is likely to see only those considered suitable to be interviewed for the position and only these are notified.

Applying for your first job

The first application for employment is always the most difficult. Nothing anyone can advise will make it easy. Even when everything is arranged, the very fact that a part of your life is being purchased needs a decision which can only be made by you. Plenty of advice and orders help to push you in what is thought to be the best direction, but if you do not like that way it will not be a very long or satisfactory employment.

If the decision is to work with horses and enough is known about the work and its employment conditions to give job-satisfaction to make it your life, take it.

How and where do you apply?

The simplest way is to collect addresses from friends and people in your own locality sufficiently interested in horses to know where a job may be found. Write, telephone or, better still, go and see these people. Do not be a nuisance, and always be polite. Several people may have to be contacted and visited before you get the first interview with somebody who may have a job. There is a purpose in your going to see prospective employers personally, of which you should be fully aware.

Job seeking

These employers appreciate an effort being made that shows the person asking them for a job wants to work with horses and can use initiative. They will also see immediately if you are suitable. Because they spend their lives judging horses to earn their living, it is natural for them to make similar quick assessments of people they may find suitable to employ.

There are several benefits from making this effort which can increase your chance of getting your first job. The costs and time should be kept low and short, and the facts and ideas which you exchange at the interviews should become clearer with each experience. Lastly, and possibly the most important of all, horse people usually ask each other about horses for sale, where they are likely to compete, and for help in time of need especially when looking for staff. Take note of any names that are suggested and always ask if you can mention the source of your information because that may be another help.

If you hope to have a job on leaving school, start to look for work and make plans for your future while you are still there. The age at which to apply to join the services and the training schemes supervised by public bodies and other details are given in their printed information. Normally you should allow a month or two to find a vacancy and another two months at least to be engaged. Local stables or studs may not have jobs to offer in the foreseeable future or your physical build and desires may make it more suitable to seek a job further afield. Letters then become the means of communication, which you will find slower, and you should write your first letters enquiring whether there is likely to be a suitable vacancy for you in the stables of your choice at least six months before you finally finish school.

Your first job and training

The schemes to give unemployed teenagers a chance to have state aid during a short trial period at the start of some training for work has affected the employment conditions slightly in studs and stables.

Now it is common practice to offer a candidate a position only on condition that he first completes a month's trial period, and, provided this is satisfactory, to continue afterwards as newly employed.

This procedure has been the method of entry into racing stables by apprentices since state education began. Working with horses, in the early part of the first year is mainly learning to be efficient and confident in the handling and riding, if that is included, of the horses and all the grooming and cleaning jobs around them. Supervision of a trainee by a competent skilled worker, especially in the foundation of the routines to make the skills become automatic and, after practise, enable the work schedule to be completed at an economic speed, costs the employer the services of the skilled person during that period. Bearing in mind the small number of staff employed by each individual stable owner − and the trainee needs at least a few months to reach the break-even standard − it is not surprising to find that owners are reluctant to have trainees who are absolute beginners.

Working pupils

The terms of employment offered for the first months on entry into a stable vary in title, duties and reward. *Apprenticeship* and *trainee* both imply that a job should be available as a fully skilled person at that place. However as a *working pupil* it is unlikely there will be one, for part of the business of a stud or stable catering for working pupils is geared to a regular intake and training programmes for them. Conditions, as you may expect, vary, but normally the employer provides food, accommodation and money for personal necessities; not a wage but enough to enable you to live through the period of training in exchange for teaching you the art of stud management or riding and stable skills. You will be expected to work as a groom maintaining and exercising any horses deemed necessary to enable you to reach the standard required to pass the British Horse Society examinations and gain your certificates.

The training received and the living conditions vary enormously and there is some exploitation of the pupils under this system, but the best places give good value. To find a suitable situation as a working pupil you and your parents should seek advice from past pupils and ensure that the claims of tuition, working hours and time off are kept, and the promised job after your training, depending if you pass satisfactorily, can be found.

31

Job seeking
Students

The term 'student', learning a craft or skill usually infers some form
of payment for tuition. This is certainly one meaning for a student of
horses, the other is the person who is studying horses as a hobby for
no immediate gain. Such people are numerous in the horse world
and adequately catered for in it. The student you may become is one
paying for accommodation and tuition, either out of your own
pocket or by way of a grant from an education or similar committee.
Again, as with the working pupil, there are no definite rules laid
down, but unless you have to work in exchange for keep and tuition
you are a student. To be able to pay for instruction in the more
advanced disciplines of equestrianism is a definite advantage, but at
the stage of entry into your first employment with horses, both
owning a horse of your own and having that independence can
remove the incentive you need to put enough effort into succeeding
to become an employable groom.

The first month at work with horses

The experience you have is unlikely to alter the conditions of
employment offered to you. Today employers select people to suit
their own requirements. You will most probably find you seem to be
at everyone's beck and call for the first few days; called upon to
sweep up, carry buckets of water and bales of straw and hay, and to
do countless other jobs you may well dislike.

Do not try to buck this system; it is necessary in order that you
may learn to fit in with the other staff in these small intimate groups
of workers including the boss who is often to be found working
alongside the team.

The value of making the effort to get some experience before you
leave school will soon be rewarded and, as you prove your worth,
the tasks will entail more responsibility and fit in well with the work
of the other staff. Later when a new recruit arrives and you are
giving orders, you will remember your first days and realise how
quickly the newcomer blends in.

The most important thing at this stage is to be working with
horses, preferably where you are learning and earning.

General points to remember

Be truthful when you give details of your experience to any prospective employer. Work with horses enables your true level of capability to be too easily assessed and if your claims of riding experience are exaggerated and believed, it is possible for you to be injured badly. Remember to tell the person in charge of your tuition and the stable management, what standard you have reached, to make sure they have the correct information.

Although studs and stables differ as widely as the horses and the people to be found round them, the actual work you will be expected to do as a trainee is an adjustment of the basic principles. Therefore it is advisable to wait until some real experience has been gained before trying to plan your career. If your first engagement is as a trainee or apprentice with job prospects at the end, complete it. Even though three years may seem a long time to you, it is not in terms of the horse industry where to breed a horse to run in the Derby takes four years from the first mating.

Training a show jumper or eventer seldom takes less than three years, and many do not reach top class until they are nine or ten years old although they start as broken-in four year olds.

The working pupil, however, may be taken on for one year or two. Some places mix the length of time and the type of people being trained. But if you are a pupil at such a place, as soon as you are sure of your aims, you should begin the search for your next job.

Letters applying for jobs

Some of the local stables may not have the person in authority readily available for you to see at a time you can call, and places some distance from your home make it senseless and expensive to travel on the off chance of an interview. The telephone can be useful as an aid to quick business but possibly a neat hand-written letter which arrives at the selected person's address with a stamped addressed envelope enclosed, will receive more attention and a more favourable reply if there is likely to be an opening to give you part-time experience or a job in the future.

The early requests for the chance to obtain working experience should be directed to arranging a suitable time for you to be seen and have any work which may be available explained to you, together with conditions of the job.

The more formal applications for employment or training under the working pupil arrangements, should contain only the essential information, which can easily be read by the prospective employer. They will not want time wasters or very long letters, preferring to decide on their own assessment when they see you.

Do not ever send by post to any prospective employer, your certificates or the original personal references, these are far too valuable to be lost. Your first letter should mention those certificates you have, and that you can supply references. However, if you have been given a letter of introduction for that specific person you should, of course, include it.

Copies of certificates and references are easy to make and most libraries, estate agents and office suppliers allow use of their photocopiers for modest payment. These copies will be needed only if you are not able to travel the distance for an interview before entering the initial trial period and are asked to send copies for your prospective employer to verify before your engagement.

While *any* work and experience is preferable to none, I personally think that a young person going a long distance from home into an unknown situation, and having to work, live and study without the comfort of knowing if the pressures become unbearable he can easily return home, may stop him from giving his first experience of working with horses a fair trial. However, later it is essential to be prepared to go anywhere a good job can be found.

Replies to your letters

The aggravation of waiting for a reply, and if one is going to come, can usually be lessened by including in all applications a stamped addressed envelope. Sometimes a postcard on which a reply to your questions can be noted saves the recipient having to write a formal letter. Stable owners and horse trainers are often loath to attend to what they regard as unimportant office work. Entries for competition, accounts for sending out, and bills to be paid, with registration and the keeping of records of breeding, have encroached on precious time more in recent years, and with the complications of VAT and PAYE, the smaller places seldom have a full-time secretary.

The following is an example of a letter which you could send while still at school.

Your full address
Date

Dear (title and name to whom addressed)

Will you have a position for a trainee groom after 30 July, when I shall be leaving school? I am 15 years 11 months, my weight is 7½ stone and I am 5 ft 3 in tall. As I am in the middle grade, the exams I am taking are all CSE, the results of which are not known until August.

All my experience has been at Mrs Smith's Riding School where I have worked in my spare time and will continue there until I leave school. I am gaining experience of mucking out, grooming and riding ponies up to jumping a 2 ft high pole.

My form master and Mrs Smith have given me references for my work and character should you require them.

I can catch a bus to be at your stables by 10.15 on weekdays, or if it is more convenient my parents could bring me on a Sunday to fix up a trial period.

Yours sincerely

To be signed in your best hand-writing

While you are helping someone in the stables or with horses it is possible that a future likely job which may suit you is mentioned. If the person who tells you about it also knows the person with that job, ask if you can give their name as an introduction, and frame your letter on the following lines.

Your full address
Date

Dear (put correct title and name of the person to whom you were told to write)

Miss Goodheart has told me that I may be suitable for the trainee groom position which you expect to have at your stables in August. All my experience with horses has been at Mrs Smith's Riding School. She has given me a written reference, but says you are welcome to telephone her for a personal recommendation, and can leave a message with her if you would like me to come to see you to arrange further details. Her telephone number is ....

Yours sincerely
Signed

As these chances are usually fairly local at this early stage of your career, the people concerned either meet or phone to exchange news and you will soon know if you have been lucky. If not, continue to keep your eyes and ears open. Never stop trying.

The advertisements in the local newspaper or horsey magazines usually require a person with experience. However not all do, and every chance must be explored. The best jobs normally give names, the others are under 'box numbers'. Again, use the similar basic rules for applying for work with horses. Make sure you write to the right person and give him his correct name and title. I stress, always ask before giving anyone's name, address and telephone number as a reference. Give your weight, height and age, the name of your school and examination results. Then your experience with horses and where it was gained. Finally try to make it easy to arrange a meeting with the prospective employer by suggesting times or places that you can attend.

Selected job advertisements

If you have had training to a fairly skilled level before you leave school, or during your initial training have discovered you have a talent for a definite aspect of work, then apart from being prepared to go to where there is a suitable job, you should state any valid reason or proven desire to enter that type of work which they are offering, as it might influence an employer in your favour.

Higher up in the job market of the horse industry, although most of the posts are advertised, personal contact and recommendation are an advantage. The normal business procedure of interviewing, after the formal applications have been analysed to select the short list, is often by-passed in the very personal world of horses and its individuals.

The advertisements also fall into a class of their own. Caution and a bit more explanation would make them easier to understand. The advertisers do not intentionally mislead the readers, but what is not mentioned may be more important than the things which are clearly stated.

A good example is 'Groom — Gardener' which may allude to a job where two children's ponies live in a paddock and only need feeding and attending to by the groom in bad weather. The rest of the time the 'gardener' part of the job is mowing lawns and tending to a huge kitchen garden.

Another common catch is 'own horse welcome' which is perfectly true, but neglects to say that there will not be time to ride it and payment for the food it eats will be taken out of your wages at market price, even if it is home grown.

The Yellow Pages telephone directory lists many riding schools, stable and studs in your area. In your search for initial work and spare time experience, look there first because they will be local. Show and sale catalogues and race programmes also give plenty of names to try.

The time at work

When you are working with horses the hours are partly dictated by nature, but the work of the horses and the staff employed with you will also be responsible for the allocation of the working hours at your place of work.

The horse has a small stomach and to get the amount of food into its system to supply the energy needed for the work means spreading out its daily meals. In most stables the first feed will be before seven o'clock in the morning, with two or three other meals equally spaced, until the staff finish work for the day at about six in the evening.

To balance the horse's requirements and allow people employed with horses an acceptable number of hours at work each week, has resulted in most of the stables following a similar pattern in normal routine. The differences, when they occur, are usually man-made or forced because of nature and work, such as the late hours in the riding school and when polo ponies have evening games to play. The breeding season on the stud farm is altered by nature from a rigid time-table.

The head person especially likes to finish to time. Regulating the timing of the staff is their duty, and as feeding and letting the horses loose to eat and rest is usually the last task, both at lunch time and after evening stables, delays then are annoying. The little extra effort you make at the start of your working life with horses, will influence the other staff to help you, but should you neglect to put in this little extra effort, you will have a rough ride and make few friends.

The normal stable routine

The early morning feed is usually given to the horses by the head groom, starting the round early enough to finish as the rest of the staff arrive. This gives the horses time to digest the food while the grooms muck out and prepare for the first exercise ride of the day. It also allows the head groom to spot any horses that have not eaten their night-time feed, which is an indication that they are not well.

In all stables and studs the time the first horses are taken out for

38

their exercise, or turned out to graze, is rigidly kept and being late seems to make the whole daily routine go wrong. Therefore, at the start of your job it is advisable to get to work early until you learn how to keep pace with the other staff. In most places you will not be expected to be capable of mucking out the normal four stables and may be given only two boxes to do before the first exercise, for a while. Because of the hustle to all be ready to 'pull-out' together, you will be told either the evening before, or find a list in the saddle-room giving the horse or horses you have to ride and get ready. The horses have to go out clean and completely saddled and bridled, so it is also necessary to make sure which they are and that you have all of their tack ready.

On the exercise rides you should expect strict supervision and instructions on how to ride the different horses in ways that are suited to them and not necessarily for your pleasure or comfort. You have to change your priorities. Before you went to work with horses you rode for enjoyment. Being paid alters the motive. Now you rely on the horses for your job and you must look after them.

The work of the horses comes roughly into three categories (1) Horses being trained for racing and competition. (2) Horses being ridden for pleasure and casual sport. (3) Breeding, dealing and showing stables and studs.

The following time-tables are examples of their normal daily routines:

Racing stable time-table

6 am   The head lad starts feeding the horses.

6.45   The staff arrive and muck out their stables and make the horses ready to ride out.

7.30   All the horses scheduled for the first lot of exercise are out and mounted, walking in single file towards the exercise gallops.

8 am   The horses gallop or canter under direction of the trainer.

8.45   The horses return to the stable and are groomed, bedded down with hay and water before being fed and let loose.

9 am   The staff have half an hour for breakfast.

9.45   The second lot of horses are on their way to the exercise gallops.

The time at work

10.15   The trainer usually directs their work on the way to race meetings.

11 am   The second lot return to the stable and are treated like the first lot.

11.30   The third lot of horses normally only require a short exercise or special treatment, which gives some of the staff time for odd jobs and tidying the stable yard.

12.30   The third lot return and are groomed, etc, less time should be needed because of the lighter work. Saddlery is cleaned and put away. Any wet exercise clothing is hung out to dry and dirty saddle cloths washed.

1 pm   The horses are all given their mid-day feed and left to eat and rest in a quiet stable yard as the staff have a three hour break.

4 pm   Evening stables. Each groom will have at least three horses to groom and get ready for inspection by the trainer. The grooming takes about half an hour for each horse, which does not include cleaning it's manger, refilling the haynet and water bucket and picking up the droppings before bedding it down for the night.

6 pm   The horses are given their evening feed and the staff's day ends.

About 10 pm the head lad will make a check on the horses to see all is well and possibly feed any difficult feeding horses. Water buckets, haynets and night rugs becoming loose can cause troubles if not put right.

The time-table of a riding school with some livery horses

8 am   All the staff arrive together and working as a team tie up the horses, giving them a small feed, straightening their rugs and brushing off dirt and damping any straw marks. Because of the numbers of horses being unequally shared between the grooms, the mucking out is another combined effort to get it done as quickly as possible.

8.45   The riding school horses are given hay and water, and remain tied up.

9 am   The grooms each make ready two of the livery horses and

take them out, riding one and leading the other. The exercise is usually a fairly brisk walk and trot round quiet roads for an hour.

10 am   The livery horses return and are quickly groomed and loosed in their stables with hay and water.

10.30   All the staff have made ready the horses needed for the riders coming for the first lesson of the day in the riding school. While some of the staff are busy in the riding school, the other grooms take out the remaining livery horses, again in pairs, for an hour. Returning in time to help with dismounting and taking the tack off the riding school horses as well as making the livery horses comfortable for their midday feed.

Noon to 3 pm   The lunch break for the staff is arranged to allow some to have extra time off and others to be early returning for the second lesson of day at 2 o'clock.

Grooming the livery horses and horses which have been used in the riding school occupies all the afternoon for grooms not required to help with clients, until about 5 o'clock, when any horses whose work has finished for the day are bedded down, hayed, watered and fed.

5 pm to 7 pm   The last riding school lessons are usually arranged to finish before 7 o'clock, but can depend on the number of times each horse has been used for a lesson. The staff are able to adjust their hours to be equal by means of a rota, which gives them afternoons off and the long lunch break on the days they work late.

The daily routine of a public stud

6.30   The stud groom begins feeding and checking the mares, foals and young horses. The grooms in charge of the stallions feed their own horses when they arrive about 6.45, mucking out the stable as the stallions feed. The stallions have to be exercised for an hour before any of the mares can be covered by them (as the mating is called) and the grooms help with finding out which mares are ready.

7 am   The rest of the stud workers arrive and commence turning out to graze the mares, foals and young horses under the

41

direction of the stud-groom. The empty stables are mucked out, either into heaps outside the doors or onto trailers. Mares which have to be tried to see if they are ready for covering are left in their stables until the stallion's grooms return. Then one of them will hold an inexpensive stallion by the trying gate to see which mares can be covered. All the grooms lead the mares in turn to this gate and afterwards help the veterinary surgeon examine any the stud-groom asks to be brought forward.

9 am   The mating takes place and the grooms have a 15 minute tea break.

9.30   The rest of the mucking out carries on and the stables are prepared for the horses being brought back in from grazing later in the day.

Noon   The stud yard should be clean and tidy. The evening feed preparation and odd jobs, such as tack cleaning and machinery maintenance will be done.

1 pm   The staff have their mid-day break.

3 pm   The afternoon work starts with fetching in the young horses for a grooming before they are fed. The mares and foals are left to graze as long as possible and usually brought in after the feeds have been put in their mangers. Other mares may need to be covered and this will be done now. The grooms will groom and inspect the mares and foals, handling the foals and picking out their feet especially, in some studs all the head collars are removed at night.

5 pm   The normal day's work is over, but on studs a 24 hour watch is kept during the breeding season and the stud-groom always makes a tour round the stables to see that all is well about 10 o'clock.

The time of the year and the weather does alter some of the routine a bit, and more alteration is caused by the horses taking part in their events.

42

Competition days

There is always extra work for all of the staff on days when some horses are going away to compete. The grooms taking the horses will need to get to work early if it is a long journey, or they may have to travel the day before, enabling the horses to be refreshed before competing.

Plaiting up the manes and tails is another skill you will have to learn and practise, for nearly all horses going into competition have their manes, if not tails, plaited. Bandages are most likely put on by the head groom for travelling to the event, while boots or bandages for the actual competition will be fitted by either the trainer or his assistant. When you are trusted to fit even the travelling bandages you are making good progress.

When it is your turn to take one of your charges off to perform, you will find the day out just as tiring as were the extra tasks left at home when somebody else went. But these breaks in the weekly routine are one of the excitements of the job and are usually shared evenly. Hearing how horses you know performed makes it very interesting and when you are telling your mates all you saw, the job is even more worthwhile.

Hunting and polo days

The horses for hunting and polo are usually stabled near to where these sports take place. The really busy days when most of the horses in the stable are used, will start earlier and finish later than normal, probably without a break. The next day will be much easier because the horses will need a rest and you should have been able to see some of the sport.

Riding schools and leisure riding stables

When people with other commitments are paying your wages, indirectly or directly, and are only able to ride at times when you would prefer not to be at work, you must have known this was to be expected before you took the job.

If you have been to a riding school or hired a horse you will know most people ride at weekends or outside normal working hours during the day. You will soon look forward to the busy weekends and light evenings with the extra activity. If you decide those are the horses you want to work among, your time off will be during the week and is better for shopping and going places; besides, the people you meet at the busy times in the stables will soon become your friends. Few horse riders can resist talking about the horses to the people who spend time working with them.

Studs

Working on a stud differs from other stables, especially during the mating and foaling season. A skilled stud hand has of course learnt the months from March to May are demanding on time. On some studs one of the duties is taking your turn to keep an all night watch on the mares likely to foal. Others employ special night watch grooms for that period only. Either way the pay is good for there is little actual work to do. When it is extra to daily duty, time off is given to make up your sleep. I always gave my staff the opportunity to sleep before their night to sit up, rather than have them fall asleep on duty. Many places allow the night watch groom to have the morning afterwards off instead.

Being at the birth of a foal which you subsequently watch grow up, and may ride and follow through its life, is most rewarding.

Weekends and days off

In general the time off at any place where horses are kept, depends largely on the way the establishment is run and the reason the horses are there.

Terms and definitions

While I believe you should have an expert to supervise your training
and instruction, I also know the jargon used by these same expert
horsemen can be very difficult to understand until you have learnt
most of the terms and names commonly used in the studs and
stables.

Parts of the horse

The important parts of the horse's body are referred to as 'points of
the horse', but the points are also the extremities of the horse, such
as its mane, tail and lower legs, thus a reddish brown bodied horse
with black mane, tail and legs below the knee and hock, is a bay with
black points.

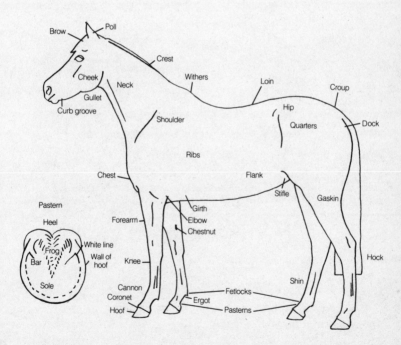

Terms and definitions

Types of horses

Horses and ponies are all able to breed when mated together, this is because they are of the same genus, height is the division and the ponies usually are those below four feet ten inches at the withers. Traditionally, horses and ponies are measured in 'hands'. A hand being four inches, thus four feet ten inches becomes fourteen hands two inches.

Breeds of horse and pony refer to the area where they originated and the work they were bred to do. Horses were always for military or work purposes until the racehorse became a special type. Now the thoroughbred, and some other named types, are bred and mixed up so much that the true origins and uses of the horses are obscure. The *thoroughbred* is normally bred for racing but can be used for almost any riding, providing you feed it correctly to regulate the energy required. *Hunters* are horses which are often a mixture of thoroughbred and the old military charger which makes a good sensible strong horse to follow hounds across country

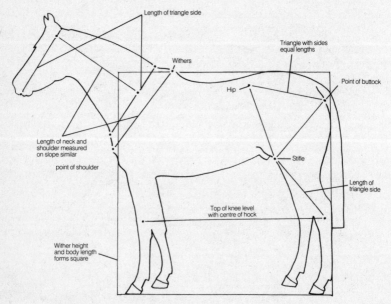

The conformation of a well made horse

astride. *Hacks* are the well-mannered lighter horses and *cobs* the tougher counterpart of the necessary run about transport before the motor car.

The anatomy of the horse gives it what is called its 'conformation'. The balance between the lengths and angles of the bones allow the horses muscles to provide different efficiency in its motive power, and any alteration in this balance can be seen in the conformation. Some gaits and actions are favoured by certain proportions which horsemen learn to measure with a practised eye, depending on their sport.

Tools used in the stable

Dandy brush — the first brush you will use on a horse will most likely be a dandy brush. The stiff bristles are good for removing dirt and scurf from the thick coats on horses who live out in paddocks, but can irritate the skin of thin coated and rugged stabled animals.

Body brush — the softer bristles of these brushes enable you to clean and massage all of the horse's coat and body. When it is used with a curry comb to keep the bristles clean, the stimulation of vigorous grooming helps to promote the horse's health and muscle tone.

Curry comb — curry combs are mainly used to clean the body brush and can be made of metal, rubber or plastic. Dried mud and burrs can be loosened or removed by a curry comb, and one or other of the types is useful to part matted and dirty hair on horses and ponies living out at grass, when you need to clean them.

Mane comb — a mane comb should only be used sparingly as the hairs of the mane and tail will break when they get caught in the teeth of the comb, try to restrict its use to pulling and plaiting manes and tails.

Water brush — dampening a mane or tail helps to train it tidily. the water brush regulates the dampness evenly and when you have to remove straw marks and dry scurf, nothing is better for the task.

Sponges — several sponges are needed by a groom and because a sponge must be clean to wash the horse's eyes, it is advisable to regularly replace the one used with a new sponge. Dirty legs, mangers and cleaning tack will soon use up the soiled ones, especially as the cheaper plastic foam sponges, which seem good to use with horses do not last.

Scraper — the removal of the excess water from the horse's coat by a scraper helps to dry it quicker, either after the horse has been out in a rainstorm or after you have shampooed or washed all the horse's coat.

Wisp — a wisp is made by twisting hay or straw into a long strand and then entwining this strand to form a pad. You can use a wisp to dry and massage, when the wisp is dampened the dust in the horse's coat comes out.

Stable rubbers — you need several rubbers in your kit, which should be laundered regularly, for they are used as saddle cloths, and for polishing and drying heels and other parts of the horse.

Hoof pick — no groom can afford to be without a hoof pick, for you have to pick the manure out of hooves before exercise and the dirt out on return to the stable, sometimes stones have to be removed during exercise.

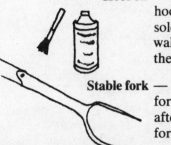

Hoof oil — a tin and brush are needed to apply hoof oil to the hooves. The frog and sole need hoof oil to stop thrush and the walls look much better cleaned and then oiled.

Stable fork — the short handled and two tined hay fork is the most used by grooms, who after practice get so used to a particular fork that their efficiency depends on it.

Yard broom — the floor of the stable and the stable yard are swept clean daily. The rubbish is usually picked up by sweeping it on to a muck-sack or sheet.

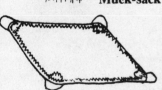

Muck-sack — an opened out bran sack was the old type of muck-sack, now a two metre square of material or plastic with handles in each corner is purchased to carry manure and loose hay and straw about the stable yard.

The wheelbarrow is used to carry heavy loads of manure and bales of hay and straw that need moving about the stable yard. A shovel may be used when a wheelbarrow is being loaded, but is not often used by grooms when they are mucking out with the muck-sheets in the stables.

Terms and definitions

Buckets, mangers and the feed bowls are obvious in their design and the hay racks and nets could not be mistaken in use, but the skep is not so well known out of stables. The skep can be metal, basket or plastic and may be used to pick up droppings or other rubbish and also serves as a container for the grooming tools, but most grooms prefer a canvas kit bag.

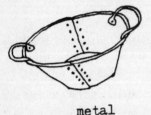 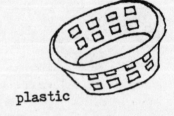

metal   plastic

Grooming a horse

A horse takes about half an hour to be properly groomed when you have learnt the method and are in regular practice.

Start by tying up the horse and putting the water bucket and hay net out of the stable, then shake up the bedding after removing any droppings so there is no dust when the horse has been cleaned.

Unfasten the rugs and inspect the horse as you remove all visible dirt, including picking out the hooves and washing them if they are muddy. Stains and straw marks where the horse has been lying down also need scrubbing with the water brush.

Fold the rugs to expose the hind quarters and with the body brush in the hand nearest the horse as you look to its rear, brush all of its coat from the loins to the hoof of that quarter of its body and leg, using smooth strokes and keeping to a rhythm which includes cleaning the brush with the curry comb. Do not forget the inside of the leg and behind the pasterns. When that quarter has been thoroughly brushed the other hind quarter can be done using the brush in the other hand. As grooming of the horse is also a form of massage for it, the strokes of the brush should go with the lie of the coat and need to be fairly vigorous. Until you get some practice the first arm used will be tired after the first quarter and you will be glad to give it a rest, this way enables you to keep working. Finish at the rear of the horse by brushing the tail with the body brush, holding

50

most of the tail in a free hand, allow about an eighth of the hair to escape, brush this with downward strokes to the end until it is clean and has no tangles, then gradually add more hair until the whole tail is together. The hairs at the top can be made to lie flat with the water brush. Now move the rugs back over the cleaned part of the horse. Again you have two quarters and legs to groom in the same fashion, leave the mane, neck and head until you have done both of these and laid the rugs over all the groomed part.

The mane tends to collect dirt and scurf, to get it out brush it both ways and especially underneath the side on which it lies. Horses have a habit of raising their heads when you try to brush their heads if they are tied up. Release the tether and be careful not to knock the back of the brush against any bone and you will find they love to have their heads rubbed. A damp water brush will help train the mane to stay tidy, occasionally a horse with scurf in its coat or mane needs the damp water brush all over as it will remove this scurf, providing the brush is only just damp. Then the brush can be swilled out and used again, unlike a damp body brush which gets clogged up by the dirt sticking to its bristles.

A final rub over with the stable rubber adds a sheen to the coat and the quarter marks and patterns to enhance the different directions of the way the hair grows can be made.

Sponging the eyes, nose, mouth and under the tail freshen up the horse and make it more alert for inspection or show, but oiling the walls and underside of the hoof puts the final touch to a well groomed horse.

Saddlery, bridles and tack

The equipment used on horses can look so different at times, yet be called by the same names, especially for its use and component parts. This probably comes about by nearly all the equipment having common origins and being evolved by individual craftsmen to satisfy needs. The basic types are illustrated to show the essential names and parts.

Most bridles rely on the horse's mouth being closed and head being held in the right position. Nose bands or cavessons as they are called have many designs and slight variations alter the names, while the basic bands hold the mouth shut by fitting round the jaw

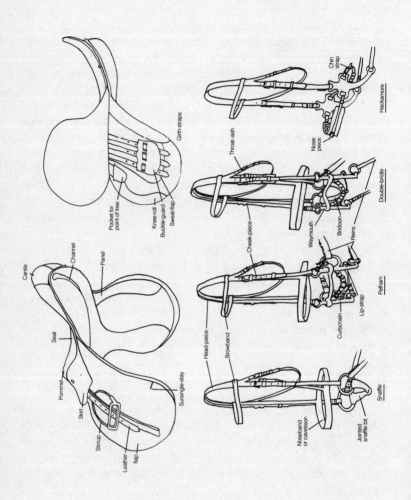

Saddle labels: Girth-straps, Pocket for point of tree, Knee-roll, Buckle-guard, Sweat-flap, Cantle, Channel, Panel, Seat, Pommel, Skirt, Stirrup, Leather, flap, Sursingle-stay

Bridle labels: Chin strap, Hackamore, Nose piece, Throat-ash, Double-bridle, Weymouth, Bridoon, Reins, Cheek-piece, Pelham, Curbchain, Lip-strap, Head-piece, Browband, Snaffle, Noseband or cavesson, Jointed snaffle bit and nose above the mouth, some have attachments or themselves fit below the bit round the mouth. The straps to position the head are called *martingales* the standing martingale is attached to the nose-band and the girth at the ends with a neck band to keep it in position. A running martingale has rings for the reins to run through to regulate the head carriage of the horse. To identify the varieties make some sketches in a note-book of all the pieces of 'tack' you see and ask how it works.

Clothing

Stabled horses are often clipped and if they are not, daily grooming makes clothing a necessity for keeping them warm in cold weather, both in the stable and at exercise or travelling.

The 'night rug' was originally used at night when the horse was allowed to lie down to rest, a 'day rug' in the owner's livery being worn while the horse stood ready for use in the stable, now they are seldom seen. New Zealand rugs are a waterproof type which allow horses to be turned out to graze without getting wet through; very useful to the owner who has to go to work and unable to exercise his horse on certain days. The night rug has become a stable rug and may have attached surcingles or a separate roller to hold it on the horse. Most rollers also have a breast girth to stop them slipping backwards, some have a high arch over the horse's back to stop them rolling over in the stable and getting stuck, this type is known as an *anti-cast-roller, cast,* being the term to denote a horse unable to get up after lying or rolling into an awkward position. The exercise and parade clothing are of similar pattern, although the weight or

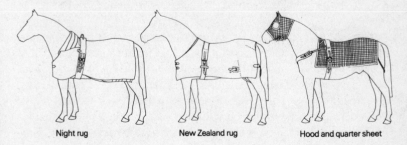

Night rug   New Zealand rug   Hood and quarter sheet

material may be different, summer clothing for the stable or travelling can also be much lighter than that used in winter.

The use of more than one rug is often necessary when a horse is clipped for the second time during the winter, and unless the exercise is going to keep them warm, obviously they will need extra clothing outside.

Bandages and boots

Horses's legs are subjected to many strains and injuries and it is often necessary to use bandages or boots to help the horse overcome them. A bandage helps stimulate an increased blood circulation through the extra warmth and gives some protection and support when correctly applied, but can be detrimental when too tight or impeding to the horse's action. The reason a bandage is being used alters its fitting, padding is used to help get a snug even fit round the limb and the tension depends on why it is being used. A travelling bandage reduces stress on the limb before and after an event by increasing warmth, support and providing protection, while the poultice bandage is slightly less tight than a bandage that must be put on the opposite leg to support it, because of the extra strain the good leg has to take when the horse rests the one which is injured. You must always try to keep the horse balanced evenly.

Bandages and boots should only be fitted when the horse has its weight on the limb if it has to move with them on otherwise they are too tight. No bandage or boot should be left on the horse longer than necessary and all need regular changing, a veterinary surgeon may request you to leave a bandage on a wound to stop bleeding for longer than the usual twice daily changing of bandages that is the rule.

The manufacture of boots for specific use has lately been aided by many of the new materials, such as plastic foam stuck on simulated leather. Over-reach boots and travelling boots with straps and buckles or velcro fastenings would be difficult to make without this new technology. The fastenings of all boots and bandages must never come undone during use and should be tested by you before they are used at speed. Sewing bandages on for competition purposes is always advisable.

The tail bandage is purely to keep the tail smart and tidy. Because it does not seem to affect any action, care must be taken that it is not put on over-tight or left on longer than absolutely necessary.

Clipping, trimming and plaiting

The horse grows a thick coat in winter to protect it from the cold, naturally when a horse is subjected to hard work this coat will make it sweat excessively, therefore to enable the horse to be used the coat is clipped with a clipping machine. The way the coat is removed, leaving the natural growth in some areas is to coincide with their work, this has resulted in names being given for the types of clip illustrated:

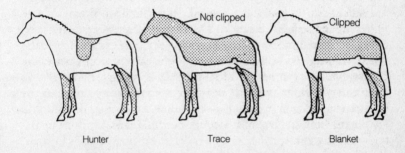

Hunter   Trace   Blanket

Clipping a horse stops the horse sweating during work and allows it to dry off quicker afterwards; it thus saves time grooming and is healthier, does not lose condition but needs clothing to protect it from the cold.

Trimming the long hair from below its fetlocks and other parts of its legs where it grows long makes drying the horse easier, and with the air being able to get to the skin fewer troubles affect the lower leg. Scissors and a comb used like the barber, makes this trimming neater.

The mane and tail are pulled to tidy. The cutting of hair in either is never permitted, with the exception of what is called *banging*, that is cutting the bottom of the tail. *Pulling* the mane is done by taking the longest hairs out when it is brushed to one side. This both thins it and makes it a uniform length, which allows it to be plaited for competition. The tail can be thinned by pulling at the top, but taking many hairs out can make it difficult to plait if this is customary.

55

Feeding the horse

The use of the horse for work means it needs a better organised plan for feeding the balance of grain and fodder, which it requires, than the farm animals who are grown to supply our food.

Because some of the food is used as energy and some for normal body functions, such as warmth and maintaining its condition, and all relies on the relatively small stomach for its size, the horse needs to have its feeding times arranged to enable it to eat and digest its food. The traditional method of giving horses hay and oats with some extra things, such as bran, linseed gruel and carrots, has been found by the recent research to be largely correct. The addition of vitamins and minerals may be needed when the basic ingredients are lacking in the amount required. Because this is often the case many horse feeders have changed to giving their horses a prepared compound feed purchased from a merchant. Hay still usually supplies the necessary bulk and all of the deficiency is made good in the compound or *concentrates* as it is called. Although horses like to have a very regular diet and even changes in the source of the hay or oats can upset them, it has still been found to be quite a good idea to give them a mash made of boiled linseed gruel mixed with bran and oats once a week.

The work the horse does during each day should be used as a guide to the amount of food it requires, because a horse working very hard needs twice the amount a horse not doing any should be given.

The actual weight of food and the further division into hay and concentrates can only be very approximate without seeing the horse, its work and the food, generally the hay will be two thirds the total weight of food for a horse used for light work, gradually the hay becomes less consumed and in proportion, as the horse becomes fitter but the total weight should increase. The following figures only apply to that horse, but show ratios: the horse standing about fifteen hands and weighing eight hundred pounds needs a total weight of good quality food of twelve pounds just to keep in condition, at light work fifteen pounds and at hard work twenty-two pounds.

The identification of the food, fodder and bedding used for horses is as important as its quantity control in the management of horses.

Hay is basically sun-cured grass, and supplies most of the bulk necessary for the stabled horse, it is very important for grooms to recognise all its forms and conditions. The best hay has a sweet smell and retains a few greenish stalks in a fairly hard and clean dry mixture. Softer hay made on meadow land, which means the stalks are thinner and shorter, is good for use on the stud farm and horses not doing hard work.

Oats are fed rolled or crushed to horses and should have the same taste as the porridge oats we eat. If they leave a sharp flavour in your mouth the horses will probably not like them either. The white middle part of the oats should form a substantial part of the grain. Being exposed to the air lessens its feed value and the milling must be regulated to allow only a week's exposure.

Barley is also a good grain to give horses and can be judged in a similar manner, although the taste is different. Feeding it to horses needs a bit more experience as they can get fat in their stomachs and develop some breathing disorders if given more than their work requires.

Bran, flaked maize, sugar-beet pulp, brewers grains and the compound mixtures as well as hay, oats and barley should be examined at the Argicultual Feed Merchants to familiarise yourself with the horse food. The time will not be wasted if you are keen to learn.

Being able to distinguish all the types of bedding is another essential for grooms because horses rarely eat wheat straw, but will eat both oat and barley straw, often to the extent of making themselves ill.

Training and education

Learning the skills necesary for you just to look after the three or four horses allotted to you in a stable yard, under the supervision of other grooms who have been there longer, and therefore assumed to be more highly skilled, but who will also be supervised by the head groom and the owner or manager of the stables, may seem a slow way to start a career with horses. But getting that early grooming and knowledge of horse behaviour is vital, because without that intimate understanding or horses, which can only be gained by being close and working with them, further learning about horses is very difficult.

The chance to rise out of the rut will depend a bit on the training you get where you work, but a lot will depend on the effort and success of further learning you make yourself. Reading about other methods of all things to do with horses and people involved in the horse industry is a very good way to begin. Everybody in the horse industry reads to learn because there is so much to know and always something fresh to hold your interest.

Once you have learnt how to ride or handle mares, foals and yearlings and organised your grooming so that only practice is needed to improve the speed at work, you should begin to learn and practise other skills which can aid promotion and responsibility.

Your place of employment governs the pay, but extra skills give more responsibility; some a little extra money; while there are others which can definitely prepare you for a wider range of work with horses and better prospects.

The duties of a groom

A groom should be able to:

— handle the horses of the stable and groom them in a routine which is safe and efficient. This includes knowing and using all the tools employed in the stable of their training:
— deal in a methodical manner with the straw, shavings, peat moss and shredded paper bedding now in common use;
— correctly fit, clean and maintain all the bridles, saddles and other

equipment used on the horses in their care, spotting any pieces that
are unsafe;
— name the 'points of the horse' and its basic anatomy and body
functions;
— recognise symptoms of ill-health and abnormal disturbances of
the horses in their care which they should report to the head groom;
— measure the hay or forage for each horse in their care;
— apply stable and travelling bandages;
— plait the mane of a horse neatly in reasonable time.

Under supervision a groom should be able to:
— exercise horses from the stable of their training or handle and
lead the animals of the stable or stud with the exception of stallions;
— mix feeds and mashes in given quantities for individual horses;
— nurse and treat sick and injured horses;
— use the form of restraints commonly employed for operations in
the stable.

During the later part of your training as you perfect these skills,
remember how the other grooms helped you and you will find your
own efficiency can improve by showing the routine to the beginners.
This is the first step towards responsibility, but the head groom or
stud groom needs to know many more things besides teaching and
supervising the grooms in the stable.

Preparing for promotion

The head groom and stud groom have similar responsibilities for
their duties in a stable or stud. In addition to discipline and the
routine timing of the stable work, they are in charge of feeding the
concentrates with any special extras for each horse, and also keeping of some stable or stud record or diary for treatments, diets and
various happenings to the horses and staff. This means they have to
learn these extra requirements of veterinary knowledge and the
dietary balance of the horses in training or for breeding.

They must be able to clip, trim and plait manes and tails to show
their horses to the best advantage and have a little farrier's skill for
times of emergency. Most stables and studs have some machinery or
appliances which they will have to keep in working order, and often

the allocation of time-off for the staff is under their control.

Education to further your career prospects

Successfully competing in one of the horse sports may be a way of being in a seemingly personal and financial position to take control of a horse enterprise. But today either an excellent proven horse master is needed as a tutor or further education can provide the knowledge and training to run it successfully. These circumstances often lead to the proprietor having to employ a manager or head person with a greater knowledge of business and horse management than he himself possesses. If you do not compete then you should endeavour to become qualified as a manager. When you select the path leading to the type of job suitable to your ability and wishes, take into account your school examination results for some courses require O or A levels.

The private establishment courses are nearly all aimed at the British Horse Society or National Pony Society horse management and instructor certificates. The advertisements in the horse and equestrian magazines supply the details of the courses offered and as most are for fee paying students or working pupils, they are not really going to further your career except by way of competition or making more personal contacts within the industry.

The agricultural colleges in the state educational system do cater for employment after their courses. Those that have horse studies and practice include in the syllabuses business studies, accountancy, secretarial skills, agricultural knowledge and other animal husbandry. The design of the course depends on the possible employment available in their area.

The variation in the subjects and the length of the courses which you can take, need further consideration. If you have passed their educational requirements, study the syllabus and inquire if you can get a grant. The grants depend on the discretion of your county education authority and whether there is an available place on the course of your choice.

Do not make a mistake and take the wrong course. The worthwhile courses are a year's hard work at least and having taken one course, a second chance is unlikely. If you are aiming to work on a stud and combine some farming in your work, do not take a course, for example, designed for horsemasters, and instructors with business studies.

The City and Guilds, RSA, Pitmans or the new BEC and TEC certificates are awarded for passes in the other subjects, but unfortunately there is not yet a universal qualification in the horse subjects at these colleges. However, some colleges give a diploma and others use the British Horse Society certificates if they are applicable.

An important factor in the formation of these courses is the involvement of the interested parties, such as future employers with professional people as lecturers.

The syllabuses for a course may change owing to demands of employment, and other county agricultural colleges may start courses suiting your needs, therefore make enquiries in your own area before writing to the one seeming to meet your requirements out of your county in the following list.

Dyfed Carmarthen Technical and Agricultural College, Carmarthen, SA31 2NH, offer a full time one year course for British Horse Society horsemastership and assistant instructor's certificates with business studies, for further particulars apply to the Principal.

Hampshire Hampshire College of Agriculture have combined with Chattis Hill Riding Centre to offer a three term course in secretarial work, home economics and animal husbandry with British Horse Society certificates, designed for girls wishing to be a farm secretary/groom instructor. Mrs J Burtenshaw, Chattis Hill Stables, Stockbridge, Hants, can supply further details.

Nottinghamshire Newark Technical College, Chauntry Park, Newark offer two courses, both are for British Horse Society certificates. The two year course is to assistant instructor with BEC or secretarial studies. The one year course is to intermediate instructor with business studies. A three year course is also available in Nottinghamshire, which includes farm business, home economics, animal husbandry, horse management and riding leading to the National Certificate in Agriculture.

For details quote the reference 276, when applying to Nottinghamshire College of Agriculture, Brackenhurst, Southwell, Nottinghamshire.

Tyne and Wear North Tyneside College of Further Education, Embleton Avenue, Wallsend have constructed courses to include

British Horse Society certificates in instructing and horsemanship to go with a variety of O and A level subjects and BEC with secretarial studies. Write to the principal for details.

Warwickshire Warwickshire College of Agriculture, Moreton Morrell, Warwickshire. Work with the British Horse Society in giving a one year course in horse management, which does require a qualification in horsemanship before you can be enrolled. The other longer courses are being redesigned and may be either a two or a three year course for management of horse enterprises. The Principal at the college will be able to tell you the entry requirements and places available.

Wiltshire The course tutor deals with all enquiries about the course at Chippenham Technical College, Cocklebury Road, Chippenham, Wiltshire, which is for training to British Horse Society assistant instructor with business and secretarial studies, but most of the students seem to find work as grooms in the surrounding hunting country.

Worcestershire Worcestershire College of Agriculture, Hindlip, Worcester, have started some short courses but as they only last a few weeks they are for people already in the industry. Write to the Principal for details.

Oxfordshire West Oxfordshire Technical College, Holloway Road, Witney, have a one year course in stud and stable husbandry with farming and business skills mainly directed for employment in the thoroughbred and racing industry.

Qualifications can be gained in farming and business management and in the secretarial and office skills, with animal husbandry and practical agriculture to make it through the options an ideal course for boys or girls. Three O levels and one year's practical knowledge are the usual requirements. The Head of the Agricultural department will be pleased to supply further details. Preference is naturally given to students who desire to make a life career in the thoroughbred and racing industry, as members of those industries helped design these courses.

The University College of Wales hold a one year post graduate course in equine studies at their college at Penglais, Aberystwyth. This is an in-depth study of nutrition, health, genetics, breeding and management of the horse for equestrians already holding a degree in one of the allied sciences.

The stables and studs

Once you have had the basic experience of working with horses, you can choose the branch of the industry which seems to offer you the most satisfactory life. To do this you should assess your own capabilities and desires to coincide with the available work and aims of the stables and studs throughout the country. The study of in-depth descriptions should help you to decide.

Riding schools

The riding school can be your first introduction to horses and ponies, but it is also very much a place of business, that is for teaching people to ride. The proprietor and staff supervise all the riding. Charges for tuition and use of the school's horses should be prominently displayed.

Until the riders are competent they are kept to docile animals in an enclosed area. The more extensive places have a covered indoor school with flood lighting to allow lessons all the year in any weather. Nearly all the better riding schools have competitions in jumping and dressage.

The Riding Club movement has boosted the business of the places with good facilities and the school's pupils and Riding Club members often combine to compete. The grooming, feeding and putting on the saddles and bridles of the riding school animals is the main work of the staff. Sometimes there is a livery stable attached to the riding school and the horses and ponies kept there will also be attended to by the school's staff.

As the staff get accustomed to regular pupils they will expect some help to tack up their mounts. These regular pupils also like to groom and feed their usual mount if possible. Mucking out, cleaning the tack and stable areas do not attract so many volunteers. Most of the trainees in the riding schools are girls, but boys are equally acceptable when there is no problem of accommodation.

The progress in riding schools is dependent on passing the British Horse Society examinations, starting in the stable management class and going on to instructor's qualifications. Some proprietors prefer only trainees with a minimum of three O levels, others are not so fussy and allow their trainees to work as grooms until they have gained sufficient experience to study for these examinations.

The riding school as an employer

Riding schools have no regulations by law which imposes minimum conditions of pay and employment to be received by the people in their stables. The British Horse Society has tried to set standards, but the best they can offer is advice on the terms employers should give the trainees and their requirements of practice. The Association of Riding School Proprietors makes further recommendations of these standards and the hourly rates for instructing pupils. Once you have passed out of the trainee level you will have to negotiate your terms of employment with your employer. Obviously it is sensible to write down these terms, and after three months you should be given a 'Contract of Employment' to comply with the law. To be legal this contract does not have to be drawn up by a solicitor, but should give clearly the following details:

Your name, when you were employed and for how long, in what capacity.

Your pay and hours of work, with holidays and arrangements for sick leave and extra benefits which are negotiated between you and your employer.

The name of the person or firm responsible to insure and pay your wages.

As a safeguard it is always better to have the value of promised fringe benefits to be calculated as money being repaid out of your wages.

The Government Act only states that riding schools have to be approved and licensed by the Local Authority to ensure proper safety precautions for clients. The British Horse Society and the National Pony Society have inspectors who see the animals, facilities and instructors conform to their standards. These inspections are sufficient to satisfy the Local Authority officials in most cases.

Unfortunately these standards do not include wages, working hours or living accommodation for employees, but many teenagers are prepared to accept a low wage and make-do food and quarters to be with the horses they love.

Instructing

The idea of teaching children and adults to ride may be attractive to you and seem a good way to make your desire to work with horses pay a better wage. The jobs which combine instructing with being a groom are in the riding schools where a profit is needed to cover the expense of keeping the animals and the upkeep of the place in addition to your wages.

Repeatedly standing in the centre of a riding school trying to get novices to perform the basic skills needed to ride the quiet ponies and horses can be very frustrating, especially if your desire is to prove how well you can ride. The hours and work are often tedious and hard, for people can only go to a riding school when they are not at work or school. Grooming and feeding after the lessons are over make late finishing in the stables the rule rather than the exception.

People taking riding lessons expect to be given clean tack and horses, and paying for an expert to teach them seems to give the idea that it is the fault of the instructor if they cannot do it properly straight away. The ability to absorb the abuse and the tears with patience and sympathy has to be in your character to teach riding at the beginning stage. Many girls, who have no ambition to compete, make teaching beginners a very rewarding and worthwhile career.

To be able to instruct at higher levels you really need to have competed successfully yourself in one of the equestrian sports, especially when the pupils are aiming to compete, which makes it a practical necessity for you to have the experience to train horse and rider in unison.

Teaching others to do things you can do is not always easy. Some people fail miserably, while others can improve their pupils to higher standards than they themselves could reach. The only way you can find out if you have the ability to teach and are equipped to stand the life is, after some practice, to put it to the test.

Private stables

The employment to be found in all the enormous range of privately owned stables can cater for every type of work with horses that is known, and although you should be very cautious of entering private stables before you are an experienced groom, some places give a thorough training and insist that you qualify under the British Horse Society or National Pony Society examination system.

There are no standard conditions of employment or minimum pay scales. The variation is from pocket money and fringe benefits to agricultural rates, or even much higher when the stable is part of a commercial enterprise. The negotiation of the terms of your 'Contract of Employment' is between you and your employer. It is even more important in these jobs to settle this satisfactorily before you start work, as in many instances you will be the only employee in the stable. Therefore, in all employment in these private stables, studs and posts with a mixture of work responsibility, you should ensure it includes the following.

Your employer's name and address.

Your name, place of work and your responsibilities with the date they begin.

The normal hours of work and the rate of pay, overtime payments and the Social Security Contributions and Employers Liability Insurance.

Holidays, normal off-duty times and, if accommodation is supplied, its use during any time you are sick or injured.

When such items as free accommodation, live as family, own room with TV, use of car on days off, or keep of your horse, have been offered or are put in the advertisement for the job, make sure that the employer includes the cash value that you will receive if they are withdrawn.

All fixed term contracts should be so stated.

This may seem like a very formal business in what is normally a friendly and personal arrangement, but it does save a lot of trouble on both sides should disagreements arise.

Private stables and hunter livery yards

The private and livery stabling for hunters is not an all the year round job, for most of the horses kept as hunters spend the summer months in the paddocks. Some employers do like to keep and look after good staff, and they will find a variety of jobs to keep them occupied from April until September. The number of horses in the stable is partly a decider in what they might do, but the places with eight or nine hunters or more are likely to have young animals to make and break during the summer. If you are not laid-off you may find yourself painting, gardening and/ or farming, especially in the yards where two of you are employed. The head person in the hunting yards is known as 'stud groom' and is a respected permanent employee.

The number of grooms employed by people hunting their own horses is estimated at upwards of two and a half thousands. The majority of the jobs are for an experienced person able to manage the horses without supervision.

Horse trials and team chasing stables

The rapid rise in popularity of horse trial riding, or eventing as it is known, team chasing and show jumping, plus the fact that it is possible to compete in all of these sports and go hunting on the same horse has widened the scope of continuous employment for the experienced groom.

The proper training facilities for both the grooms and horses are still only to be found at the larger establishments run on a sound business method, which enables them to pay reasonable wages and reward service.

The opportunities to compete or learn more than exercising horses will be restricted in most private stables, where horses are kept by people who wish to compete themselves. Many of these stables do allow you to keep a horse as part of your pay, and getting a horse to improve your riding is a good way to make progress. Even though the extra training is usually outside working hours the effort is worthwhile and supplies the way for the ambitious.

The exercising of the horses is an important item in most of these stables. The older hunters are usually quiet, but you should have the experience to ride the more lively horses being prepared for competitions.

Polo

The work with polo ponies is a summer-time occupation. Occasionally a club or team keep a skeleton staff on during the winter, but again it is work for skilled grooms. The exercise and preparing the ponies, as they are called, (although most are big enough to be termed horses) for playing the matches is all regulated to a rigid schedule and does not allow time to train any unskilled workers. Playing polo matches has to be at a time when the owners can get away from their business which is usually at weekends and in the evenings. Even their riding practice is done at odd times so early and late starting and finishing in the stables is normal for the grooms who are nearly all girls. There are few chances of promotion, but it has a good social life and much travelling to compensate for the hard work and long hours. The best prospects are with the players who take their ponies abroad, sometimes for a long tour in a team.

Trekking centres and riding holiday hotels

The boom in horse riding has brought thousands of casual riders to enjoy the pleasure of riding quietly in the countryside. The chance to travel the old tracks away from built-up areas and main roads on horse-back at leisure; besides making owning a trekking centre or riding holiday hotel a good business to be in, has turned the operators into the largest employers of seasonally engaged grooms and riding instructors in the last few years.

The hotel and guest houses who offer horse riding as part of their attraction, often want the grooms to help with other duties in running them. This is an advantage for wages and for staying longer. Plenty are separately owned hotels to the stables and only operate together to help each other's business.

Another rapid growth has been in the summer vacation camps for school children. The adventure programme frequently includes pony riding, and the organisers regard employing grooms qualified to instruct as giving them a paid holiday for the summer months.

The tourist boards soon realised the necessity to ensure the safety of the thousands of people flocking to take holidays on horseback. Societies have been formed in England, Scotland and Wales to advise on correctly conducting the riders, on insurance and suitable ponies. Their concern has resulted in special training courses for Trekleaders to instruct them in managing the inexperienced riders with safety, some First-Aid, and special care of the ponies is also given. Because of the demand, these courses are held in the Spring and early booking is advised. Their duration alters but usually some charge is made and they include practical trekking rides. The two societies most likely to help find work of this type are those in Scotland and Wales. Again, please enclose a stamped addressed envelope for a reply.

For places in England you may write to are:

The English Riding Holiday and Trekking Association c/o Approvals Office, The British Horse Society, British Equestrian Centre, Kenilworth, Warwickshire, CV8 2LR.

For Scotland:

The Scottish Trekking and Riding Association, Tomnacailn Farm, Trochry, Dunkeld, Perthshire.

and Wales:

The Pony Trekking and Riding Society of Wales, 32 North Parade, Aberystwyth, Dyfed, Wales.

Recruitment starts many months in advance of the time you will be wanted at any of these holiday and seasonal jobs, but occasionally an isolated cancellation may result in a vacancy during their busy period. Reading the advertisements in the horse and pony magazines is the best way to find a suitable job in the area you desire, but don't forget that in order to instruct or be a Trek-leader you will need qualifications or to pass their course.

For information about the work with horses at a PCL Young Adventure Centre the address is:

Personnel Officer, *PCL Young Adventure Ltd,* Boreatton Park, Baschurch, Shrewsbury, Shropshire.

Show jumping and eventing stables

To be a groom working for a rider of international standard has a lot of glamour attached to it. You will also see many show grounds or large country estates, and some visits overseas may be part of the yearly travelling. The social life and meeting famous people is only a very small part of how the days are occupied, for the horses have to be exercised and groomed to perfection for their public appearances. Living in the motor horse box's cramped quarters, while trying to keep the horses fed and stabled comfortably, is very difficult when the performances are at irregular times.

Returning to the home stables is not a rest during the competition season, it is merely a time to clean and polish everything and load up for the next trip. The riders cannot afford to pay for sufficient grooms and certainly have not the room to carry them or time to train anyone. The expense of entering and transporting the horses to the shows seldom make a profit, and the sponsors, necessary to bear the cost of maintaining the horses needed by a rider to stay at the top today, have accountants who cut out luxuries. The acceptance of the inconvenience of the long walks between the horse box, the stables and the show jumping ring is only one of the things you will have to bear at the show grounds should you decide to learn the skills needed to join this growing band of dedicated workers.

Plaiting the manes and tails has to be quick and neat. Cleaning the bridles and saddles speedily and being able to put on bandages efficiently, all need a lot of practice to perfect. The ability to sleep and put up with meals at odd times while going to shows is an asset. The eventing or horse trials' competitors (to give them their proper title) do not have quite the same intensive campaigns in public, but that does not lessen the qualities of their grooms, which are similar when they do go to compete.

However, to get a job of this type you will have first to become proficient and then wait, while keeping in touch with the grooms of the riders, until one of the grooms leaves, because there is fierce competition for them and the number employed small.

Hunt service

The people employed in the kennels and stables, where the hounds are kept, enjoy special privileges for the work they do in providing the sport for the followers. These include the provision of nearby accommodation for both married and single people, and continuous full time jobs at roughly the current agricultural rates of pay.

70

In addition, there are perks and the traditional Christmas box, which is collected at one of the best 'meets' by a cap being taken round to all the followers and spectators – who are generous towards the 'hunt servants' – and later shared out in proportion to their jobs and length of service. While you should not expect to get rich by going into hunt service, you get the chance to be paid to do something everyone else counts a privilege and pay a great deal to enjoy.

There is a special Hunt Servant Benefit Society Scheme which is a good idea to join if you make this a career, for it covers you in case of accidents and sickness with help at retirement and cash if severely injured.

In Britain, four hundred people are in hunt service with the one hundred and ninety six packs of fox hounds, and about one hundred and seventy more work with the harriers, beagles, drag and stag hounds, mainly in the hunt and masters' stables. Service in the larger hunts has a slight distinction between the workers who ride and those called the dismounted staff. The latter are kennelmen and earthstoppers or terriermen who have little to do with the horses. The huntsmen, whippers-in, second horsemen and grooms all have to ride and in the smaller packs will also do all the other duties.

Because the work means being among a particular crowd of country folk and does invoke its own principles, I think you should follow the hounds on a bicycle, if you cannot ride by reason of expense, and talk to the staff and followers whenever possible, before you decide to make this your life. Entry into the stables is open to all grooms who can ride, of any age or sex, preferably below a weight of eleven stone seven pounds and, as most of the exercise is trotting along country lanes, the ability to ride one horse and lead another is an advantage, but as the hunt servants' horses are by necessity well mannered and quiet, it is fairly easy to learn. You would soon see some of the action because there are seldom enough grooms to take the second horse along for the master and the servants to change onto at the half way stage of a day's hunting. Taking the tired ones home after their hard work to make them clean and comfortable before the second lot return, and then having to set about another batch of wet and muddy horses is the hardest part of the job and does make the hunting day fairly long. Most packs hunt three or even four days each week from November until the crops begin to grow on the farmland in late March or later, cub hunting starting at first light in September and the parades of the hounds at the horse shows does not allow much slack time for the staff.

Hound exercise and the whipping-in duties are often combined with the grooms' jobs, but the more specialised kennel work is thought by most of the Masters of Foxhounds to be suitable only for men, mainly because of the need to collect the 'flesh' of dead horses, cattle, sheep and pigs to feed to the hounds. The skinning and cutting up of the carcasses can be unsavoury and does need both a strong arm and stomach, besides strength to pick it up off the farms in the lorry most hunts keep for that purpose. The best time to look for work in the stables is late summer, but for the skilled hunt servants the foxhunting year begins on the First of May and most changes of staff and forthcoming vacancies are known by Christmas. The honorary secretary of the Master of Foxhounds Association keeps a hunt servants' register of all the staff and requires from staff who wish to be on it, their places of employment, experience and a current reference, which is very helpful because he finds and recommends staff.

To obtain the registration form and further details, you should write to: A H B Hart, Hon Sec, MFH Association, Parsloes Cottage, Bagendon, Cirencester, Gloucestershire.

Please do not write if you are still untrained as a groom and rider, and if you are qualified to make enquiries, do remember that Mr Hart is unpaid and can only reply if you send a stamped addressed envelope.

Seasonal jobs and fixed periods of employment

Some grooms enjoy the change in their work at regular times in the year, going from a quiet country life with hunters in the winter to the mad dash of the show-jumping circuits or social life of polo stables. It does add to the excitement of living and it is possible to maintain full employment all the year round with a variety of horses and people. The snag, if you consider it one, is that experience has to replace any formal training, and promotion opportunities will not be those earned by service. However, it is often ambition that spurs a person to try to get out of the settled and organised rut. Most people plan to achieve success. The extra experiences may suit their character and enable them to learn more about horses in this manner.

Another way horses and ponies may spark your ambitions, when you are working with them, is by watching them give others enjoyment after your training. The desire to have horses and stables of your own soon mounts and while the saving of cash requires real dedication, it is possible to achieve even at a low level in the horse world. Many of the proprietors of the small livery yards started off by being penniless grooms, then saving to buy a young horse to school in their spare time and sell on at a good profit, eventually being able to rent stables to house horses belonging to customers they met while employed.

Which is the best way for you to succeed is not a question I can begin to answer, for there are too many examples of the various paths which horses have taken people on their way to a happy and successful life with them. But I can tell you that all started with good basic training in stable management, so get that before anything else, then you can use it to advantage.

Racing stables

The flat racing under Jockey Club rules is the popular concept of racing, mainly due to the press and television coverage of the sport for its betting. Flat racing and the jumping of steeplechase and hurdle races all come into the same category which may be termed 'professional horse-racing'. All the other racing of horses, such as point-to-pointing, Arab Horse Society races, and the pony, galloway or flapping race meetings are either amateur or do not come into a recognised code of practice.

Flat racing

The light weights carried on the flat by the horses has led most people to believe that only small very light boys are able to go into racing stables. Stories in the newspapers about some of these lads becoming successful apprentice jockeys, because they have been riding winners handicapped to carry less weight than the established senior jockeys can manage, has furthered this belief. It is partly true for at one time all the flat race trainers took several undersized boys from city centres each year in the hope of finding another Gordon Richards or similar famous jockey from that background. The wastage of a year or two in the lives of these fourteen years old boys did not cause them harm and many are still working in racing. The system also helped many others without family connections in racing to start their careers because the trainers fed and clothed them, which after the smog and smoke of the cities the life in the country with a disciplined purpose opened their eyes to a new world.

Few trainers try to make jockeys in this fashion now the school leaving age is sixteen and, as the rules decree, full wages to trained staff at eighteen, there is also the problem of teaching them to ride and look after three expensive race horses in the two years; something not many can do in that short time.

Today, boys and girls must be able to ride and groom horses before being accepted as a trainee. The apprentice jockeys still can emerge eventually from the trainees, but it takes them until their late teens or help from someone while they are school children.

Most flat race horses are young because the races are for mainly two and three year old horses. All thoroughbreds are given the First of January as their birthday to simplify their age for racing, thus every one born this year becomes a yearling next January and those now yearlings become two year olds. Light riders on the backs of these immature horses are necessary for their exercising and galloping, some start being ridden when they are really fifteen or sixteen months old.

Boys should be about six stone at the age of sixteen, but girls can be a little heavier. The trainers seldom allow any regular exercise rider to be more than nine stone, and imposing these weight restrictions seems to enable the grooms to have a better chance of a lengthy employment. However, work in racing stables is not confined to the flat.

Steeplechasing and mixed yards

The horses which race over hurdles and fences are older and stronger because of this and the heavier weights that are carried by them, so too are most of the staff and jockeys employed to ride the horses to exercise, both older and stronger. Jockeys can continue riding in races over jumps when they get too heavy for flatraces, amateurs are allowed to ride over the jumps and many of the jockeys now riding started that way. Learning the art of jumping at speed in the hunting field is good for horse and rider, then experience of race riding in point-to-points or hunter races helps the young amateur jockey get mounts. As this method needs some financial backing it is usually a boy from a family with connections in racing or farming who is given the opportunity. After winning enough races while riding as an amateur a change to professional jockey is made.

The training of flat racers and jumpers is possible in the same stable yard, and many of the smaller trainers have what is called a mixed string. A mixed string means the horses can either race on the flat, over jumps or some may even run in both types of race. The staff can be as varied as the horses.

75

Racing yards in general

Learning the art of being a good stable worker takes time. The jobs
and standard of skill attained by the grooms are defined by the
employers and not subject to any examination or service qualifications, (with the exception of serving an apprenticeship to be a
jockey, which also means you learn to be a groom.) The Jockey
Club rules and the competitive contact between the employers has
evolved a system of exchanging truthful information, on a personal
level, about grooms and stable staff when they apply for jobs.
Trainers normally telephone your last employer before offering you
an interview, the rules do not allow them to engage anyone who has
worked in racing stables until they have received satisfactory
references from their last employer in racing. The system also
extends to racing jobs abroad, so you should always expect your
capabilities to be known at a new job before you arrive.

Should you feel that your abilities could enable you to take some
responsibility above an ordinary groom and exercise rider, but do
not fancy trying to be a jockey there are plenty of opportunities for
promotion to be found. The first jobs which give extra responsibility
are being a travelling head lad, (who is in charge of the horses going
to the race meetings) and assistant head lad (the head lad is in
charge of the horses and stable yard in the absence of the trainer),
helping with the feeding, veterinary dressing or supervising some
tidying or cleaning tack.

Lester Piggott was once a lad in his father's yard in Lambourn and
still had to 'do his horses' after riding the Derby winner. Barry Hills
is only one of the stable boys who have eventually become famous
trainers. Nearly all the real professional people in racing began in
the stables, grooming and riding horses out to exercise two or three
times every morning to learn thoroughly all the peculiarities of race
horses and racing.

The early morning start is the traditional way for the routine to be
arranged. It does enable the trainers and jockeys to be on the
gallops before they dash off to the race meetings and keeps the
horses away from the flies and very hot sun in the summer.
Originally it was thought early morning mists prevented onlookers
from seeing how the horses were galloping. The staff have a break
from noon until tea-time and once you get used to this break, it is an

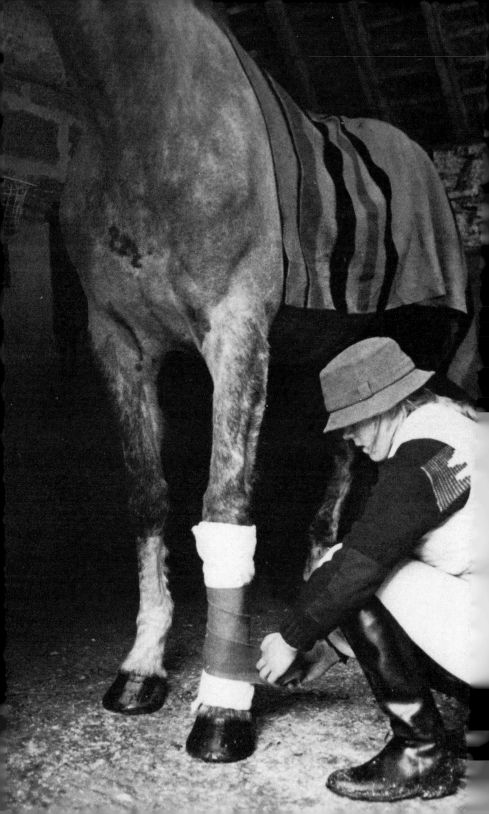

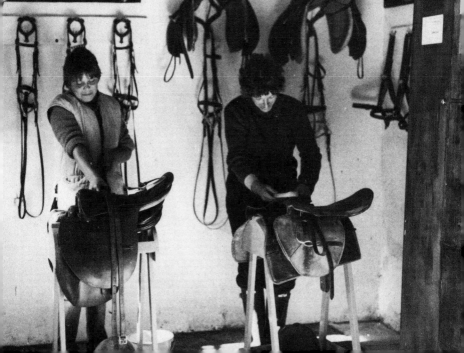

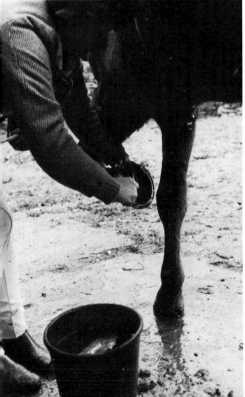

easy and convenient way to live.

Science in horsemanship and husbandry, as with everything, is progressing and my own view is that trainers and headgrooms will soon have to study to take formal qualifications before they are granted licences. The money side of the sport will bring this pressure and already some racing countries abroad and a few agricultural colleges here are beginning to offer courses on feeding and training race horses.

The Jockey Club licenses and registers all the people employed in racing. One of its rules makes the paying of minimum wages to stable staff a condition of the trainers holding their 'licence to train'.

The wages and conditions of employment in racing

To understand how racing alone of the horse industry comes to have a statutory minimum wage needs a little explanation. Starting with the flat racing apprentices who were taken into the yards each year, there had been a fairly high turnover of cheap labour to be absorbed by all racing stables as these apprentices became trained grooms. The winter's break from flat racing pushed the larger grooms into jumping and the once five months' close down of jumping in the summer, ensured the studs and stables had enough skilled men for the seasonal work with the mares and foals and for breaking-in the yearlings. Some unrest was caused by raising the school leaving age and the rate of inflation altering the perks and traditional living standards of the grooms. In 1976 some strikes and the formation of a Stable Lads Association enabled the basis to be negotiated for a minimum pay scale.

The National Joint Council for Stable Staff formed in 1979 reached an agreement with the Trainers Federation to pay fifty per cent of the minimum wage to sixteen year olds, sixty five per cent to seventeen year olds and eighty per cent to eighteen year olds with less then twelve month's service in a trainers' yard, for a forty hour week and a standard five hours overtime at weekends.

The grooms in some stable yards had been used to having alternate weekends free and receiving a standard wage each week, so the basic pay was for this forty five hour week but the lads only worked two weekends and then had the third one off.

The trainers agreed to pay the expenses at standard rates for lads

77

taking horses away to race, especially overnight and the late returns from evening meetings.

Perks have always been a large part of the stable lads' income above the basic pay. The introduction of a two and a half percentage of the prize money being given to the groom or stable staff has meant fewer ready money handouts, but the prize fund, from which this share is taken, has nearly doubled in the last three years. Each year the minimum wage of the racing groom has improved and is about the agricultural rate, the perks and the four weeks holiday make it an attractive job for a single person, the responsibilities of marriage often coincide with those at work or settling down and making the job more secure. The employers like married people in the most important jobs and provide houses for them.

The secretary of the Stable Lad's Association, Tommy Delaney, reviewed the situation of work and pay in the stables as follows:

'Conditions have altered rapidly by the extra horses in training and fewer staff to look after them. Maintaining the race-horses at peak fitness and in a healthy state cannot be achieved by shorter exercising and grooming. Each lad can look after and ride out only three horses a day, extra riders may help with exercising; then just the grooming is curtailed, when the lads have five or six horses each to do, and even more on race days. Horses are usually taken to the races by their lads leaving extra to groom at home.

'The head lad comes under more pressure, for in addition to checking all the horses in the absence of the trainer, he has the normal duty of supervising the staff, feeding and dressing wounds and injuries to contend with. Should he also have to groom some horses the standard of work falls. Training staff under these circumstances is very difficult.'

Tommy Delaney, who, like his father and brothers, started in racing as an apprentice before riding as a jockey, and being a head lad at Epsom and Lambourn stables, suggests all people wishing to enter racing should become efficient grooms and riders before seeking a job with a trainer.

The jobs are there because the resulting figures from a questionnaire to all trainers revealed that three thousand are now trying to perform the labour intensive work of four thousand skilled stable employees of a decade ago, and as training horses has not altered, it must be people to do the work who are missing. In addition, about two hundred and fifty sixteen year olds are needed as an annual intake, subsequently only half of these will stay in racing as a career, after spending two years in the stables.

Another future worry for the industry will be inexperienced staff to replace most of the head lads and senior responsible staff when the remainder of those trained under the old apprenticeship system retire. Because at the moment Britain has not managed to ensure the back-up training to a level possible before, the few taking courses in feeding and management in horse husbandry besides those who are enticed abroad, are insufficient for the studs and stables.

Because of the lack of grooms in France a few years ago, many British racing grooms crossed the Channel. Now that supply has stopped the French Ministry of Agriculture evolved a combined school and work programme to maintain a regular flow of recruits into their racing stables and stud farms.

The collected views of racing overseas shows the British trained racing groom or head person can always find a job in France, Germany and Italy. There is also a shortage of exercise riders in the places where racing is maintained by importing the horses. In Singapore, Hong Kong, Cyprus and the Scandinavian countries many grooms have enjoyed careers as jockeys after being unable to get any mounts on the race courses here.

Apprentice riding courses

The courses are free for all accepted pupils, and last for seven weeks, at *The Apprentice School*, Goodwood Stables, Chichester, Sussex, PO18 0PX. There are six courses each year which are open to boys and girls, but as an interview cannot be arranged more than six months before you are able to leave school do not apply until just before that date.

You will be taught how to ride and look after a horse in the correct manner, and learn some elementary stable management. Providing you can gain enough proficiency a job will then be found with a licensed trainer. The conditions of acceptance on the course require boys to weigh less than seven stone and girls may weigh up to eight stone, be in good health and produce a doctor's certificate at their interview. They also require a letter from your headmaster saying you have average intelligence, and you would have to state if you had any convictions in a Juvenile Court.

At the present time The Betting Levy Board, which helps to pay for these courses in conjuction with The Jockey Club, is trying to find larger premises to expand the number of pupils trained each year on the courses. Should you receive no reply to a letter addressed to *The Apprentice School* either The Betting Levy Board 17-23 Southampton Row, London, WC1B 5HH or The Jockey Club, 42 Portman Square, London W1H 0AP would forward a letter.

The Armed Forces

The horses used by the armed forces are mainly for ceremonial purposes. There are a few pack animals and riding horses used in the remote stations for supplies and communication, but these are usually privately owned and used for convenience.

Officers and other ranks are encouraged to keep horses for recreation and competition, especially abroad, where the stables are often attached to the station. Racing, horse trials and show-jumping ranges from pure novice riding to competition at inter-national level. The events won by the members of a unit of the forces gives as much boost to the unit as its other sports teams. To judge from the Military Meeting at Sandown Park race course, and the various point-to-point races held at Tweesledown and other places, horse trials and jumping shows are helped by the Services and some rely entirely on Army organisation to be held.

There are a great many equestrians in the forces and, as in civilian life, the horses require grooms to attend to their needs.

The Royal Army Veterinary Corps, Equestrian Wing, at its depot at Melton Mowbray, Leicestershire, runs courses for officers and other ranks in the horse troops, which teach all aspects of riding, feeding, training and horse management. The horses needed as replacements at the two ceremonial units usually pass through the wing as remounts, as they term unschooled horses.

The ceremonial units of the Army using horses

The Household Cavalry and the Royal Horse Artillery, Kings Troop, are both based in London. To serve in either is regarded as an honour, and although you would be re-taught from scratch, it is obviously much easier to gain admittance to these élite postings if you have had some experience.

The officers at Kings Troops, St John's Wood, and the Cavalry Barracks at Knightsbridge are regular or short service commis-sioned soldiers trained to lead men in the normal modern fighting mechanised units of the Army and because of the great esteem of a tour of duty in either place, are usually restricted to a three year stay.

The Armed Forces

The troopers in the Household Cavalry are in The Horse Guards or Life Guards and have to undergo the basic training of the soldiers of a light armoured regiment. Because only about two hundred are needed at a time from the regiments, you have to be selected to serve on ceremonial duty while the rest of the regiment carries on as a normal part of the Army. A high academic standard is not required, but to join the Guards you need to be over five feet eight inches tall and weigh upwards of a hundred and thirty pounds with a physical fitness to pass the medical.

The gunners of the Royal Horse Artillery are also members of a fighting regiment and when not serving in the privileged King's Troop may be posted to other stations. There are about as many places for a tour of duty with the ceremonial guns as in the Guards, but the height and weight minimums are lower which allows slightly more competition from recruits.

Applications to join either of these highly esteemed and superbly drilled horse ceremonial units should be made before your seventeenth birthday, as there are more applicants than places. The details and current Commanding Officer's name and address is available at your nearest Army Recruiting Office.

When you write it is advisable to include any reason why you believe your training, ability or family background suits you to be enlisted. An invitation is usually given to prospective recruits to spend a few days at the barracks and in the stables to really understand all the special demands you would have to meet if you joined their ranks. The first step towards receiving that invitation depends on the effort you make to show them you are a suitable candidate.

Being in the armed forces in peace time enables you to get extra tuition and facilities for any sport. Leave and training time also is usually easier to get. These privileges include the equestrian sports and, as a bonus, the use of the best horses from those performing the parade duties is quite often encouraged, together with transport for a team.

82

The Mounted Police

The mounted policemen and women who give the displays at the Agricultural Shows and control the crowds in some of our cities are policemen and women combining ordinary training with that of being a mounted officer.

Several years of being a 'bobby on the beat' has gone before the hard extra training to make them into the splendid commanding figures riding the well disciplined fearless horses needed to perform in a manner we all respect. To become a mounted police officer you will first have to want to be an ordinary constable, because all the nineteen police authorities with a mounted branch, insist on the completion of two years as a constable on normal duties before entering one of the police equestrian training schools for the six months' hard work of learning the stable management and riding techniques necessary for mounted duty.

There is a written examination which must be passed and, of course, a medical examination with minimum height regulations usually about five feet six inches or more for men and slightly less for women. Because of the time the horses have to carry a mounted officer on duty, the authorities seldom allow any officer to undergo training who will be over eleven stone before they are twenty five years old. While novices and recruits all begin together to learn how to ride and groom, it is easier to make faster progress when you have already had some experience of horses and riding.

The attraction of the dual roles of 'riding officers', as the police call them, brings more applications than places and so there can be no promise that you will be allowed to ride a horse on duty. It is therefore advisable to go into the police force only if both being a copper and working with horses are equal ambitions, then should you fail to join the mounted ranks you can ride when off duty. Most of the forces with some riding officers have facilities for recreational riding by other officers. Formal applications to join the Police Force have to be made to the Police Authority of the city or county where you desire to work, but by making a friend of your local bobby, you can get him to enquire where your best opportunity may be to join with the hope of having a career as a mounted officer of the law.

Studs

Stud farms in general

The purpose of the stud farm is to breed horses and ponies. Because of the restriction imposed by nature most of the foals are born in late spring or summer-time. Tradition and our once dependence on horses has led us to believe that horses need help to mate and produce foals eleven months afterwards. With the expensive thoroughbreds and some others, not native to these islands, people being in attendance at these times is really a safeguard for the animals which cost so much money. The native ponies manage quite well without interference.

The extension of a riding, hunting or racing establishment to include the occasional brood mare with a foal at foot is not a stud in the true sense of its meaning. Such places though, are often an ideal way of getting an introduction to the knowledge a skilled stud worker needs.

Commercial studs

Breeding horses for sale, and looking after other people's breeding horses to make an annual profit, is an easy way to define commercial studs. The inclusion of a stallion to mate with mares brought to visit him, for a fee, turns it into what is termed 'a public stud' because the stallion is being offered on the public market for serving breeding foals.

The private studs do not have a stallion for public use, and while some have other people's mares, they normally send the mares kept there to a public stud to be covered by a stallion, but sell the foal or keep it as the owner's desire, not having mares from other studs to visit the stallion keeps it private.

The size of the commercial stud can vary from those similar to the National Stud where Mill Reef and Grundy stand (both valued at about two million pounds) down to the small studs producing very moderate foals.

Not all of the studs are those with acres of lush green paddocks, well posted and railed, surrounding a country house and some smart buildings which are full of sleek coated mares and foals in the spring and summer. Some are only part of a larger farming enterprise, and others are tucked away behind tall hedges with cottages and few buildings on less than a dozen acres. In common, they will all have ordinary men and women working on them, mucking out and carrying bales of hay and straw as needed, while feeding and turning out to graze and then catching the horses later to put back in the stables for the night. The work is much the same as in the riding stables if you substitute turning out for tacking up and catching for grooming after exercise.

The value of the animals they breed and the standard of work expected of the staff does bear resemblance from the top down to those producing just below average priced yearlings. You can judge from the staff if the place is improving or not. A staff too small and not having the time or trouble to keep the animals and place clean and orderly is a bad sign. Even in the Arab, show horse and pony studs maintained by their owners private incomes, the success of the stud is reflected by these same things, which are a relative indication of the value of the horses being bred there.

The entry into employment on a stud can be as a general labourer without previous experience of horses, but as such it is doubtful if you will have very much to do with the horses, because there are always fork and broom jobs to muck out the stables onto the trailers, driving the tractor to harrow paddocks, repair fencing and haul supplies of hay and straw.

When you have decided you want to work with horses, but are not able to compete and really would not enjoy grooming and exercising horses everyday for people who do, think about stud work. Producing, rearing and even the breaking-in and early training is done on some studs.

The wages are normally about the agricultural rate with bonuses for good sales and overtime when the foals are being born, and at most weekends during the covering season. Accommodation is often provided nearby or you are helped to find it. The work is very interesting and because it does not receive the same publicity as the competitive sports, is often forgotten, although the most essential, and often rewarding work with horses for someone dedicated to a life with them. Then if you have had some practice of handling, riding and grooming your first job in a stud should be aimed at working with the horses and learning all the duties of a skilled stud person. There will still be the mucking out and other hard work, but you should also be assisting with handling foals, yearlings, and the stallions and mares at breeding times, taking and collecting horses from their home studs or to the sales, and meeting people who are customers of the stud. A successful stud is seldom without some activity or visitors.

To become a competent stud hand ready to move to the best promotional opportunity, you must find a good commercial public stud and be prepared to stay three or four years to experience a thorough variation of the seasons which affect the breeding of expensive horses. The esteem of the 'stud groom' and prestige of the stud does have a value to all your future employment as you will find if you make this your career, because later you will be asked 'where did you learn stud work?'. Employers put most merit to that initial training.

Your age and size do not matter when you wish to go into stud work, but health, ability and above all else consistency do, for you will be a vital person in a small dedicated team which you must not let down.

Some of you may be able to have a taste of the stud life by working for an employer who combines a working stable with a stud farm. Not many of these are large enough to be entirely separate. Usually the stud will have its own stud groom and the stables of the ridden horses controlled by the head person, with some change of other staff between both places as the work demands. If you are lucky enough to be given such an opportunity, take it because it is an excellent way for a young groom to get an insight to a future career.

Many of the agricultural colleges have realised the career possibilities of the stud farms attached to farm and business enter-prises, and are holding courses for students who may already be working on a stud or are going to make breeding horses their life's work. The British Horse Society and the National Pony Society also have stud management courses with diplomas and certificates, but these are more for the owner-breeder and less commercial people.

A small stud of those breeding show or native ponies may not have an income sufficient to employ someone all the year round or even full-time, but as the work is skilled and demanding (besides the fact that to breed horses of no value would be stupid) occasional jobs can be found on them. Many of the studs of this type are family or egoistic ventures and offer a mixed responsibility type of employment. An experienced stud hand might find himself washing a car, getting a load of logs, feeding cattle, digging potatoes and minding the children, between putting the mares in their paddocks and getting them in at night. You may be happy doing this as many people already are. It can supply a long and fulfilling span in your life, the only drawback being that there can never be any prospect of promotion.

World travels in stud work

The prospect of getting a job abroad is probably greater for a skilled stud hand or groom, if you are sufficiently experienced with horses below competition level, because of the huge exchange of bloodstock for breeding internationally. There is an almost weekly traffic in horses between the major countries famous for breeding race horses, (such as Britain, Ireland, France, Italy, Australia, New Zealand, Argentina, Venezuala and the United States of America) and sometimes the new owners offer their grooms the chance to travel and settle the horses in their new homes. That is not much extra expense when you consider international stallions cost over a million pounds.

The seasons on a stud

The busy foaling and mating time on the stud starts in February and lasts until June. The hard work and bustle of the long hours of attending to the mares with their foals are soon rewarded by watching the spindle legged foals dashing about the fresh green paddocks and having to splay their forelegs to bite the short new grass.

Summer is usually pleasant and holidays need to be taken while the horses spend longer out in the paddocks. Odd jobs such as painting and repairing are the order, before the barns need cleaning out for the next year's supplies to be brought in.

The autumn of the bloodstock world is one time when everybody seems to travel and move animals about, this is partly because all the major sales of the yearlings, bred for racing, take place then, and because there is not the need to keep the twenty four hour watch on the mares likely to foal. After the yearling sales come the sales of breeding stock and some foals who are mainly bought by studs to prepare as yearlings for the next year's yearling sale. Also the horses which have finished their useful careers racing for the owners who bought them as yearlings or bred them. Some of these become the stallions and broodmares of future seasons.

The places where jobs are going to be available and who can fill these posts is one of the topics of conversation at the bloodstock sales. Most of the changes in employment in the commercial studs, from the top jobs as manager of a stud with two or three stallions with a hundred mares on a hundred acres, down to lads coming out of racing yards and wanting to start work on a stud, are often first discussed at the sales by the interested people. Travelling and meeting are simplified by the horse boxes bringing and taking the horses, enabling grooms to get lifts, while few of the employers can afford to stay away from these important places of business.

To get overall experience as a stud hand who hopes to become a stud groom or manager, the public stud offers the best prospects, for in addition to the duties of attending mares being mated by the stallions, there is the chance of assisting with a greater number of mares foaling and the care of foals that may require nursing.

The public studs, because of having a larger staff required for the visiting mares, have also improved their facilities to include foaling units so that they can act as a maternity hospital for horses. Some have closed circuit television to watch the mares without disturbing them, and most have a clinically clean surgery attached to the specially built extra large foaling boxes, with their little room where the attendant grooms spend the night when necessary.

Harness horses

All horses used to pull carts, implements and other loads are collectively known as harness horses. There is little use for pack horses or mules in Britain today, other than the Highland pony to carry the carcass of the deer shot by the stalkers in Scotland.

Trotting and harness racing

The sport of trotting is widely practised on the Continent and in Scandinavia but has never gained much popularity here. In America the trotters and pacers rival the galloping race horses as a spectator sport, and are a vast source of employment similar to that in some parts of Europe.

Light harness horses

In Britain, the use of ponies and hackneys is for show and personal pleasure. There is a certain amount of employment to be found by specialist people who have learnt the art of driving in an amateur capacity but I advise you to seek work of this nature only as an extension to the normal stable duties of a groom, unless, of course, your employer is willing and skilled enough to train you in this art. When you are proficient in driving and training harness horses, then work can easily be found either in the show or racing circles.

Heavy horses

The public attraction and advertising value of heavy horses has brought many Shires and Percherons back on to the streets in England. The Clydesdales are commonly to be seen in the northern counties and Scotland, in the city of Aberdeen they have recently been brought back to work for the city council. The Suffolk Punch has spread across from East Anglia to Cheshire, where both they and shires can be seen as working horses again in central England.

No agricultural show would be complete without several teams of heavy horses trundling their huge wagons round the ring. The ploughing competitions are similar with horses decked out in dark coloured leather and brass harness, showing off the 'master carter's' art to perfection.

The popularity of these heavy horses, and the work available through their reintroduction by firms for publicity, has been increased by these firms finding deliveries were costing less money while retaining efficiency. Consequently many more firms are investigating the use of horses again for short journeys. The fuel crises and high prices have also helped to favour the horse.

To illustrate the number of horses coming back into this work, my saddler has been asked to help find six strong young men to be apprenticed to a Master Saddler just to make the heavy horse harness. The scheme has the backing of a nationally known firm who keep horses themselves.

The work in the stables with these gentle giants is possibly easier than with riding horses because many are stabled in stalls and all the muck is dropped behind them in one place. Feeding and grooming should take about the same time as for a riding horse on working days, but preparation for a show or display will mean getting to the stable in the small hours to wash and polish the horses and the harness. The plaiting up is a work of art and different to the type used on saddle horses and the 'feathers', as the hairy lower leg is called, have to be washed and dried before the horse can travel in the horse box. Putting the harness on these horses is fairly easy once you have the knack, but it is heavy and, as some horses stand six feet high at the shoulder, getting the awkward bulky collar over their head and turning it round on the thin part of their neck is not a task for a five feet tall weakling. However, as working with the horses is only part of the job, the other part is delivering the goods of the firm, being strong enough to load and unload the goods will govern whether or not you can do a carter's work as well as utilizing your horsemanship.

The wages will be similar to the other delivery men employed by the firm, with overtime for weekend work with the horses. Should you want to find a job with these beautiful animals I suggest you either follow them back to their stables and get an introduction through the stable boss, or note the names and address on the vehicle they pull and write to the personnel officer to ask what prospects there are of getting a job with that firm.

Farriers

The farrier is the person who shoes horses and other jobs he may do are really blacksmith's iron work, like making wrought iron gates or mending the farmer's ploughs and harrows. Today it is more likely he will come to the stable to shoe the horses carrying a portable forge in his van, to enable him to alter the shoes and fit the shoes hot or cold, as required. The village smithy or forge has disappeared in most parts of the country but, like the saddler, the farrier has benefitted from the fresh use of the horse for leisure purposes, and seems to have his future assured.

Shoeing horses

The art and technique of making and fitting shoes on the horse's hoof is very skilled work. Watching the master farrier work may make it look easy, but one of the nails going too far into the hoof can ruin the horse and if they are not in far enough, or the shoe and hoof do not match, the shoe will come off fairly quickly as the horse moves about.

The art takes a few years to perfect and because there were not enough farriers at the start of the boom in horse usage, many unskilled people tried to set up as farriers. Now all farriers must be registered to be able to legally carry out their trade.

Learning farriery

To become a farrier you have to find a master farrier who will take you on as an apprentice and teach you the techniques. This is not as easy as you might expect because not all of the two thousand registered farriers have the facilities required by the National Master Farriers and Blacksmiths Association for the teaching of apprentices.

If you cannot find a place yourself The Farrier Apprenticeship Scheme, administered by the Council for Small Industries in Rural Areas (CoSIRA for short) may be able to advise you where there is a future vacancy.

After a probationary period, you should discuss with the master farrier your entry into the Farrier Apprenticeship Scheme.

This scheme is grant aided and the rules forbid any contract of employment being entered into by applicants before the place on the scheme is approved. *The Farriers Registration Council*, 4 Royal College Street, London NW1 0TU, or the Master Farriers and Blacksmith's Association at 674 Lofthouse Lane, Wakefield, Yorkshire sometimes know of farriers willing to take on an apprentice. Do not forget to enclose a stamped addressed envelope.

To be apprenticed you should be between sixteen and nineteen years of age, and to have shown an aptitude for farriery, so metal work should be taken at school and you should also start looking for a place before finishing school. Living away from home might be necessary during the apprenticeship.

The courses in farriery are at the *Hereford Technical College*, Folly Lane, Hereford HR1 1LS under the tutor, Mr T F Williams, and the Diploma of the Worshipful Company of Farriers examinations are taken in the final year.

For further details if you are resident in England write to: Senior Crafts Officer, *CoSIRA*, 141 Castle Street, Salisbury, Wiltshire SP1 3TP.

Applications from residents in Scotland should be made to : *Scottish Development Agency*, Small Business Division, 102 Telford Road, Edinburgh EH4 2NP.

Residents in Wales should write to: *Welsh Development Agency*, Small Business Unit, Treforest Industrial Estate, Pontypridd, Glamorgan CF37 5UT.

Saddlers

The master craftsman who makes saddles and harness for horses is a very skilled person, and should not be confused with the seller of saddlery and leather goods.

The saddler

To become a saddler you will have to be apprenticed to a member of the Society of Master Saddlers, and learn all the skills needed in this much revived trade. It is difficult to find a master saddler willing to take on an apprentice but if you are persistent and start learning how to stitch leather, and are willing to work in exchange for being shown something of the craft, eventually you may find one to take you on. Probably you will need to live near to his shop and take the year's course in saddlery at the *Cordwainers Technical College*, Mare Street, London.

The secretary of the *Society of Master Saddlers*, 9 St Thomas Street, London SE1, or the bursar at the Cordwainers college can sometimes answer letters about available jobs, provided you enclose a stamped addressed envelope.

Many of the people taking up repairing saddlery and harness are trained grooms, as a working knowledge of the use of the things being repaired is essential. When designing and making the new pieces of harness, and a saddle to fit a horse and the rider, it is even more vital. Harness for driving horses in wagons and carts is harder and making the collars for the heavy horses is very specialised work for strong men.

Should you find an apprenticeship to a saddler, expect to be asked to sign on for three years and in addition to attend the Cordwainers course. Then on completion you will be expected to stay with your 'master' for another two years on full pay.

The popularity of things made out of leather and the demand for saddlery and harness, and the repairs, have brought a boom in the trade of the saddler's shop. The craftsmen behind it are finding it difficult to keep up with the work, therefore it must be a craft with good career prospects.

Veterinary nurses or dressers

The qualified veterinary nurse is highly trained and needs to be based near to a college where the qualifying courses are held during training. However, most veterinary surgeons employ people as handlers and dressers for the animals visiting the surgery for treatment, and afterwards in the kennels and stables. Most of these nurses or dressers have no formal qualification, but the length of service with a veterinary surgeon will be counted and backed by a reference when you move to a job with another practising vet. To find work with horses only your vet employer would have to have a large horse practice, but some vets do specialise and others keep horses for pleasure, so it is possible to find work of this sort whether for a boy or a girl. Girls may find it easier as they can also be used as receptionists and secretaries.

Occasionally the universities with a veterinary school take students on a working pupil basis to train as veterinary nurses. They do ask for O and A levels and expect you to gain qualifications. Most of the universities now have stables and the following addresses may be of help:

Bristol University School of Veterinary Science, Park Row, Bristol 1.

Cambridge University School of Veterinary Medicine, The Old Schools, Cambridge CG2.

Edinburgh University Royal (Dick) School of Veterinary Studies, Summerhall, Edinburgh.

Glasgow University Faculty of Veterinary Medicine, Bearsden, Glasgow G61 1QH.

Liverpool University Faculty of Veterinary Science, Abercromby Square, PO Box 147, Liverpool.

London University Royal Veterinary College, Royal College Street, Camden Town, London NW1.

See also under the British Equine Veterinary Association.

Where will you live?

It is never convenient to live far from the stable or stud where you work. You will be lucky to find a permanent job with subsequent promotion close to your present home, so at some period everyone working with horses has to go where the horses are, or stay in a rut.

Once you have found a job which you can accept, ask your employer for help in finding accommodation, if it is not provided. Most good employers ensure staff working with their horses have adequate living quarters. Do not make do. If the hostel is bad, tell the boss and ask for improvements or a room with someone who takes lodgers. Even as a working pupil or apprentice you have a right to the pleasure of properly cooked food and the comfort of a dry bed and clean clothes.

Self-catering accommodation with several other staff of the same sex in a cottage or a caravan may be fun in the summer, but in cold weather while you are trying to learn and work, your turn to cook, wash your clothes, and clean the place out and keep it warm will not be an adventure, it will be hard work after being out all day. If that is the only place available make sure you get properly organised before there is any bad weather. Do not let your health suffer by neglecting your food or your sleep.

The necessity of open country for animals means stables and studs are usually in a country area. Cinemas, disco halls and youth clubs are not usually found close by or even within nightly travelling distance. Therefore you often spend the early days working with horses in the company of the people you work with, even when you are not at work.

Later you will set your own living standards and possibly be influenced, when you decide upon a new job by the living accommodation available. This is good because the type of accommodation offered does show how much an employer respects the staff.

Horses attract many wealthy people, among them a few rogues of both sexes. Even when some of these may be friends with your boss be cautious of the offer of parties or a night out seemingly for nothing.

Part-time work with horses

The spare time jobs with horses on a regular basis are more likely to be found in a horsey area. Someone who keeps a horse for a hobby and as a means of getting exercise himself, often does not have enough work to warrant employing a full-time groom, but welcomes the chance to employ a dependable groom at certain times during the week and is prepared to pay for both help with exercise and stable work at those regular times.

There is also a demand for temporary full-time work with horses. Several agencies advertise in the equestrian magazines for grooms able to take the filling-in jobs, for such times as when a person is on holiday or injured. For example an instructor-groom I know keeps two horses of her own and earns the money to pay all their expenses by going out to other people's stables to work between 9 and 4 o'clock, the regular schedule she keeps begins at 6 o'clock every weekday and often ends at 7 o'clock at night, having mucked out, groomed and given riding lessons or whatever her clients required, while travelling about fifty miles on her moped. She is doing something she loves, and believes her efforts to keep and school her own horses for competition are eventually going to give sufficient reward.

Another one has made a business of plaiting and preparing animals for the horse shows in summer and clipping them for hunting in the winter. Then there is the jockey who, when he does not get many mounts, supplements his income by rasping the sharp edges on horses' teeth.

There are also seasonal jobs such as preparing yearlings for the sales, and travelling grooms for summer shows. The specialised work does need experience and usually the responsible trained groom is the one wanted. Pay for your services as a temporary groom, exercise rider or whatever special talent is yours to offer, will be higher than long term jobs, but the employers in these situations are more critical and will not let people without proof of experience, and references from previous satisfied employers, into their stable or stud.

Taking a job abroad

The offer of a job in a foreign country has a certain amount of glamour attached to it. But before doing anything about such work read this chapter carefully. An increasing number of British trained grooms are taking the jobs advertised by the agents of the foreign employers in this country and are being interviewed and engaged on behalf of the employers by the agents before being sent to the stables and studs to work where they find conditions are nothing like those they had been promised.

Most of the work is well paid and there are good opportunities with a highly respected employer who keeps the promised conditions of employment, and expects the British grooms and horse management to be of a similar high standard. However, when you take a job abroad with horses you must have a return ticket or the money for one and it is advisable to have a contract before you travel. While the risk of a private employer having a fatal accident or going broke is always present working with horses, you need these extra precautions to safeguard against being stranded a long way from home, possibly through illness, injury or simply by losing your job. To enjoy working in a foreign country with horses you should have completed your training and had plenty of riding experience. These are the essential qualities looked for in British grooms by foreign employers. Do not spoil that reputation and high regard by impatience and indiscretion, although it is more likely that only you will be the loser with a bad job in awful conditions.

Many countries have regulations to stop foreigners taking the work away from the native people, and as a foreigner you would have to get a 'work permit'. In America and many other countries, including some of the European countries this permit is valid only for the job you travel to take. Should you become unemployed you are not allowed to take another job in that country unless you have arranged to make the move well in advance of leaving the first one. Once you lose the protection of the official work permit you are in that country illegally and can be deported. The British Consul may sometimes help pay the fare home and smooth out any rough treatment by the foreign police, but the money will have to be repaid, eventually.

The British Health and Social Services may not cover you when you are working out of this country, and you must take out your own insurance to cover hospital and doctors' bills in case of illness and accidents. The possibility of the necessity to return home should also be included.

The customs and local laws can be interpreted better by someone who has had first hand experience of working in a similar situation in the actual area where you have been offered a job. Therefore find someone who can give you these details from their own personal knowledge, before you finalise a contract to work in a foreign country, even for a short period. When the job is in a country which is not English speaking, it is important to learn the language sufficiently to enable you to talk to the local people, for you will have to deal with them in getting your own personal requirements for living, and even in stables catering for English speaking tourists, the local people will most likely supply some of the goods and services. If the job includes travelling with the horses in that country, it will be necessary to be able to talk and understand the people you come into contact with on the journeys. The treatment and feeding of the horses can be different to our traditional ways. The religion of the country and the dependence of the native population on horses for work, food or pleasure alters the way horses are handled and stabled. The method of feeding often has to be adjusted to cater for the crops available. Few countries grow crops specially for horses, like the farmers here and in the USA. This may also affect the food you will have to eat too.

The climate of the country often changes your routine, the clothes you wear and your way of living as it does that of the horses and your work with them. The standard of living accommodation and the treatment of workers by the authorities can be very different. Especially noticeable will be the attitude of foreigners and even British men to the working girl once they are abroad. The factors which influence these changes in human behaviour cannot be simply explained, but an interview in an office in this country will not tell you the problems you may encounter in the stables or on the stud overseas.

The agent offering the job should be able to put you in touch with some person who has been employed in that country, but you can make your own enquiries starting with a reference from the prospective employer at the Embassy for his country in London. You will have to visit that Embassy anyway for the work permit and probably an entry visa. Even if the agent promises to do all the paper work it is a good idea to go and get some of the details of their requirements and the conditions of the country for yourself. The agent should also be able to tell you which Bloodstock agency is negotiating the job, which Transport company the employer uses or is known by. Either way a discreet phone call should supply you with the answers to these important questions.

The world is small when you need information about people owning horses but is huge if you are stranded miles from home in a foreign country. Finally if you have any doubts at all, whether it is references, terms of the employment contract, or your insurance cover, seek the advice of a solicitor before you sign the contract or travel. Such advice is not necessarily expensive and can save much trouble in the future.

Future jobs after being a groom

The experience of being a groom is never wasted, but it is foolish to stay a groom when you have lost the zest for being with horses all the time, and the future starts to worry you. It is normal for such things as increasing weight, your health, or injuries from accidents, to force a change in what work you can do. But before this happens or, better still, if you have doubts about your ability to progress in your work with horses, you should consider adding another skill to your experience as a groom.

There are now excellent facilities to enable you to have further education in most subjects which can open up a whole new range of jobs to you when added to your knowledge of horses and the people in the industry.

Secretarial and book-keeping

The office work on a stud, or needed in the ordinary stable, is seldom enough for a full-time secretary. The combination of knowing about work with horses and being office trained, increases your value to the boss. Better office jobs will also become available as you become experienced and known to people with whom you are dealing on behalf of your employer, such as horse auctioneers, the horse transport firms, bloodstock agents and even larger establishments in the same type of business with the horses.

Selling horse requisites

The mature reliable person who has worked with horses seems to be able to find a job fairly easily selling any of the horse requisites and clothing for horse and riders. Working in a saddlery shop, or for the feed merchant, or travelling round the shows or stables with equine veterinary preparations and feed additives may not seem to require much knowledge of horses to you, but the customers can be influenced in their purchases by a salesperson who can advise them from genuine personal experience. While companies who offer these selling and travelling jobs always say training is needed to sell their goods, what is true is that selling to people in the horse industry does need practice and having contacts and being able to discuss the value of the goods being offered in terms the buyer and seller both understand is most important.

To relate your own talents to the most rewarding selling job is not too difficult. For instance, it will be easier to talk to customers when you can understand the chemicals in the mixtures if you are selling medicines. A few years buying hay and straw as a head groom teaches you the value of foodstuff, and as a merchant has to both buy and sell, an assistant who has been a head groom should suit him.

The horse transport firms prefer to employ drivers who have been grooms, not because grooms are good drivers, but they understand the importance of giving the horses a comfortable journey and can help avoid trouble with loading and unloading, which is the time when most accidents occur to the horse. The international transport of horses is a full-time job for the companies handling the traffic. Airlifts of horse cargo have not increased during the last few years – remaining at about five hundred horses each year to all parts of the world – however road transport using the sea-ferries has grown and exported horses sold through the bloodstock agencies (which are the only figures available) accounts for two and a half thousand leaving this island. The long distances and high insurance make the employment of expert grooms a necessity to travel with these valuable horses.

The horse artist

The paintings and photographs of horses and riders are usually improved by the artist studying the action and anatomy of the subject. Stubbs, one of our most famous artists, started by drawing the bones and muscles of dissected animals before painting his horse masterpieces. Photography has helped with actions in the paintings and has developed as an art itself.

Study of painting and drawing must have talent to complete the paintings. Photographs too need skill to arrange a better composition than those taken by customers themselves. Selling your work brings you success and satisfaction.

The sculpture of horses is becoming very popular. Even with the gift of natural ability, practise to perfect likenesses or saleable forms takes years. But recently prices obtained by young sculptors for 'realistic' works gives hope that more will try to join them.

The horse event reporter/journalist

In order to write about the events, horses and people involved in the sport and industry in an attractive manner, it helps to have been actively part of the scene for some of your working life. Most of the readers of the racing sales and show reports and articles are people with connections and interests in the industry. The use of jargon they understand makes better reading to them and keeps up the sales of the publication.

Further education

Full or part-time education in a technical college is available to every one over the age of sixteen years. When sufficient O levels have not been gained it is possible to make them up by further education, either part-time if you are working or full-time if you have not found a job. Choosing the subjects which can help in a future career obviously needs careful thought to blend them with your existing skills and qualifications.

The courses usually start in September and the head teacher in all state schools has a list of the courses planned for the county. Seeing the list and asking advice may give you help in planning your future.

The local education authority of your area is responsible for grants and the allocation of places for schooling and retraining, and while most vocational courses are free to persons under eighteen years, checking and obtaining the current availability of courses, grants and living allowances and any costs which may be required, is something only you can do. The system is there for your education; please use it.

Manufacturing craft

Building stables and making horse boxes, trailers and the carts and wagons for them to pull, or any other ancillary equipment usually depends on some trade or craft similarly learnt to an apprenticeship with horses, but is often enhanced by a better finished article after training in the new skills following your work with horses.

Money and horses

The source of money in the horse industry

The method of making money, or where the money comes from to pay your wages, is a very important consideration in any job. In a widely spread and often privately sponsored industry with its individual employers, it is better for you to plan your career with horses armed with the knowledge of the different factors which influence the various branches of the horse world.

Normally, any industry relies on selling its goods or services to customers. With horses, some of the profit has to be measured by the pleasure the person footing the bill is receiving, especially in hunting and amateur sports. The professional sports and those catering or offering a service to paying customers are usually run on ordinary business lines.

The point at which your work becomes profitable for your employer can vary with the type of training and establishment. Bonuses over the usual basic rates paid to grooms can only come from profits.

Profit and bonuses

Profits for owners and bonuses for workers in the horse industry only come from wins and successes by the horses. It may be from a race, a show jumping contest, the prize at a show, the price above that expected in the sale ring, or even someone who has been pleased to have a comfortable ride on a well mannered horse and, as a token of their pleasure, gives the groom attending the horse the price of a drink in the local pub.

Success and fame in the competitive field of horses is normally only a few years, often during your twenties. Of course there are many examples of people carrying on longer, but generally these are the best years in competitive sports to make money, and it is advisable to start investing early in your career in whatever long term horse business you intend to continue.

Do not make the mistake of thinking the glamour of working with expensive and famous horses can alter the true fundamentals of today's harsh financial business world. Mortgages, tax and keeping accurate account of expenses and earnings need attending to amidst the excitement.

Racing

The money to buy the horses and keep them in the trainer's yard until they can win races comes from the owners. This includes the wages of all the staff and the living expenses and things the trainers have to pay for to stay in business. Not many of the horses can win enough to cover their annual training bills or to increase their value to make a profit for the owner when they are sold after their racing days are over.

The fascination of trying to own a horse good enough to win any race is sufficient to keep most of the owners paying the bills. The very rich or famous people aim their horses at the prestige races, such as the Derby and Grand National. Fortunes are spent every year, far in excess of the prize money, buying and paying training bills by the owners, in the hope that their horse will bring them fame and fortune.

The daily newspapers give a lot of space to the race programmes and the prices of the most expensive horses. Much of the information they give is connected to the chances of certain horses to win the next big race or how the horse managed to win afterwards. Usually this includes the owner, trainer and jockey getting publicity − not much notice is taken of its groom. However trainers and the stable staff get a ten per cent share of prizes, so success can reap a handsome profit to add to your wages.

The winners of the big races usually come from the best stables with good owners and a loyal staff of experienced people. The ability of a trainer to produce more winners or raise the class of race his horses win, will attract both more owners wanting their horses in the yard and more grooms seeking to work in a successful stable. Therefore, it is natural for them to choose carefully their horses and the grooms to help train them.

Gambling

Obviously if you are going to work in a racing stable, gambling on the races will be constantly mixed up in your life. Whether you like to bet or not is your affair, but any information you may glean as a result of your work should never be divulged outside the stable.

Some of the owners of horses you meet may be bookmakers, but remember they depend on racing taking place for their business, and inside information about the horses can swell their profit, whereas if the trainer found out you had given away stable secrets, sacking you stops the leak and makes finding another good job for you in racing very difficult.

The prize money

Flat racing has really two sources of income, apart from the owners. The prizes constitute the first of these and in addition to the amount supplied by the Betting Levy, some comes from the race course admission, sponsors of races, television fees and the entrance fees of the horses paid by owners. Secondly and by far the most valuable is the worth of the horses after winning good races to be used for breeding.

Steeplechasing and hurdling relies solely on its prize money and supporters.

Breeding thoroughbreds

The studs run on commercial lines produce yearlings to sell at annual sales. Just over three thousand yearlings find buyers each year at auction, another fifteen hundred go into training after private deals, or maybe have been bred to race by their owners. Some very wealthy owners maintain studs in their endeavour to win the 'classics' as the Derby, Oaks, Guineas and St Leger are known.

Some landowners and farmers breed horses as a hobby and these can vary from top class to hunters, but many of the best steeplechasers were born on farms.

Other horse breeders

Most of the breeders of ponies, hunters and Arab horses regard their studs as a hobby. Some are purely business ventures and make good profits supplying top class animals for both the home and export market. The show ring is used as a shop window by the breeders of these animals. Few have performance tests and conformation is the method of judging value. Thousands of pounds are given by wealthy people trying to buy ponies and horses able to win at the numerous horse shows, all over Britain, just in the breed and young stock classes. The prestige and the extra buyers for other animals bred or produced by these people must pay, for there is little money to be won.

Dealing and training horses

The specialised trainers of horses in the mainly amateur sports, such as polo, show jumping and horse trials (eventing) usually buy and sell for clients, as well as deal in horses on their own account. Sponsorship and the boom in equestrian sports has brought more money into holding the competitions as public entertainment. Now there is a growing number of successful riders who have found it possible to train riders and horses for the events in which they made their names. Not all have retired from competitive riding or have turned professional in that sport, although their stables are established as a commercial enterprise making them money.

The success of National teams in International competition, with the Royal family keenly interested and taking part in eventing, polo, driving and show jumping, has attracted publicity and participants who have transformed these equestrian activities from country gentlemen's pursuits into the crowd pulling entertainment now very profitable to stage. Badminton has about a quarter of a million spectators each year and the week of The Horse Of The Year Show at Wembley has all the seats booked months in advance. Prize money at these indoor jumping shows has risen to over ten thousand pounds for each sponsored class, and international show jumping horses are being sold for fifty thousand pounds, more than the best steeplechasers, who, like them, are mostly geldings and have no breeding value after retirement. Plenty of dealers and people who started riding for pleasure are making their living by buying young horses to school as hunters, eventers and any other sport where they have experience of the type of horse required. Some just trade, while others keep horses at livery as well.

Livery yards

The origin of the livery yards began when the horse was the only means of travelling about the country quickly. Travellers could hire a horse at one yard and ride to the next, changing their mount for a fresh horse, leaving the tired one to be returned after rest by someone going the other way. Today the livery yard is a place where people without stables can board the horses they own, paying a weekly fee for keep and exercise.

Trekking and riding schools

You may envy the life of the people working at the riding school or at the holiday centre where you have been trekking, but to provide the horses and facilities for use by all the customers, it must be an organised business. The proprietors have an all the year round job. The capital interest of the property and horses, together with the wages of the staff and cost of keeping the horses, insurances and other things necessary to run the place, are all added up. Then after complicated calculations it is possible to arrive at the charges, based on the hourly or weekly hiring time by the customers of each horse, that the proprietors need to make for an overall annual profit.

Mixtures in studs and stables

Because there is such a variation in the requirements of people and their horses, many different forms of transactions and arrangements can be found in the dealings of the horse world. Riding schools may be in part a livery yard, or have some horses to hire out to competent riders, or take horses to break-in and school for competition. Private studs and stables can have just as many mixtures of horses owned and being paid for by people other than the proprietor of the establishment, depending on their knowledge and experience of their paid staff.

Putting money into horses

Investing large sums of money in a horse enterprise or buying expensive horses before you have some practical experience is not a wise idea. The peculiarities and economics of the horse industry has many changeable factors. The best way to study the influences affecting valuations and the demands of the fluctuations of the market, is to work with horses under a steady trustworthy employer who has been in the business for some years.

There are always wealthy people who are attracted by the glamour of the life, and publicity surrounding famous horses, that they will spend a fortune to be part of it, but seldom does their money satisfy their wishes. Higher than normal wages or super conditions of work, with erratic promises and behaviour by the management, should be viewed with caution, especially in the early stages of your career. Training with horses needs to be continuous. Not working to schedules and being unsure of your boss's requirements because of the lack of supervision and direction, can be as distracting as the worry of having to find another job.

Incomes from services for horses

The farrier is usually a self employed person and has established a number of clients who require his services on a regular basis. The charge for shoeing a horse is calculated on time, skill and materials used, plus the cost of the journey if the work is done at your stables. Most of the master farriers employ trainees or skilled workers.

Saddlery, hay, straw and feed marketing, supplying requisites for equines, and riding gear cannot be separated out from everyday trade, but over four thousand firms specialise in supplying and making things for the horse market. Veterinaries too, treat and prescribe for domestic pets and farm animals as well as attending to horses when required. To help provide a constant service, with a qualified vet on call twenty four hours a day, usually each practice has partners and younger newly qualified assistants. The British Equine Veterinary Association has seven hundred members and about four hundred of these specialise in treating horses.

Several Auctioneers sell only horses, some like Tattersalls of Newmarket concentrate on thoroughbreds and others like Russell Baldwin and Bright are official auctioneers to the Hunters Improvement Society and the National Pony Society. Altogether twelve auctioneering firms rely on horse sales for their livelihood.

Transporting horses and being shipping and dealing agents supports many people in the industry, so I would say there is plenty of money to be earned working with horses, but first you should get the training and experience to make the most of your opportunities to reap the rewards effort brings.

Professional competition and self-employment

The chance to make your fortune working with horses happens to only a few people and depends largely on luck and singular personal ability. Until you have tried to make your mark in the particular sport in which you believe you could make horses perform better than those professionals you have seen (or could do with a bit of practice), there is always a chance that you could be one of the few.

Unfortunately it is impossible to forecast when or if ever you will become either rich or famous. Some chances have to be taken in any competitive sport, especially when horses are being ridden or driven. Being able to get a living wage while you are helping to train the horses gives you a very big advantage because you will be getting advice from the top professional jockeys, show-jumpers, polo-players or whatever sport the horses you are working with are engaged in.

The decision you will have to make while you are young enough to take full advantage of the opportunities, which only those of you in a competition stable have, is whether you believe you have the ability, dedication and courage to stick to a rigid programme of training mapped out by yourself to achieve your ambitions.

Do not make a hurried decision because it is not necessary. Time to breed, rear and train horses is matched by a similar time it will take you to get properly trained and ready for a competitive career with horses.

Once you have made your mind up, do not become frustrated by the obstacles which seem to get in your way. Rarely is a famous horse rider young. It will have taken many years of hard work to reach that standard of horsemanship and fame.

The risk of not getting to a similar position should never stop you from trying, because the effort will not be wasted while you are with horses. The ambition either to compete or have horses to train yourself seems to be sparked off by watching the horses, ridden at exercise and groomed by you, performing in public, ridden and instructed by others, leaving you only as a spectator and determined to alter this situation.

To have your own horses and stables is a possible achievement after making the effort to learn the stable management and enough about competition riding and training to be trusted to have care of other people's horses. Many of the proprietors of the livery yards and, indeed, all the stables financed by people working with horses as a profession, started by taking a few stables or saving to buy a young horse to school for sale in their spare time, eventually renting a stable yard and collecting customers from among the owners met while employed.

There is no restriction on how far working with horses can take you if you are prepared to work, study and use the industry as a help.

Livery stable proprietor

The stable which relies on customers' horses being boarded, fed and exercised and groomed there for its weekly income is a form of livery yard. The Jockey Club licensed trainer and the girl who lets children keep their ponies in her stables or field for three pounds a week are both making an income from liveries, although they may be offended if you told them so.

The object of that comparison was to show the range and possibilities of becoming self-employed after thoroughly learning the horse husbandry.

To run a livery stable and any small stud or training yard, you should have learnt to feed, ride, groom, clip and break horses because the early days are the most difficult. In addition you need to keep proper books and records, repair saddlery and the buildings, handle customers with a quiet personality, unshaken by long hours of work, bad weather and people not keeping to the arrangements.

Once over the initial period of about a year to eighteen months, you should have some permanent guests or regular customers to allow you to invest in a young horse to break and school for sale. To enjoy the life and make it profitable this is the natural thing to do, and it is most rewarding.

Organisations in the industry

The horse industry has connections with many offshoots – everything from foundry and finance, through food, drugs and chemicals, to leather and textiles. While it is better to write directly to the prospective employer, sometimes you will need help to find one. In the following list of organisations with comments on their roles in the industry, some people are mentioned who may have information from employers with vacancies:

The Animal Health Trust
Lanwades Hall, Kennett, Nr Newmarket, Suffolk.
This Trust carries out research in the veterinary science of problems directly affecting the horse. Scholarships and Fellowships are awarded when a practical and immediate need is indicated by field investigation.

The Association of British Riding Schools
Chesham House, 56 Green End Road, Sawtry, Huntingdon, Cambridgeshire PE17 5UY.
The proprietors of the riding schools founded this association to formulate policies in management, standards and charges affecting their business.

The Bloodstock and Racehorse Industries Confederation Ltd
St Agnes Cottage, Bury Road, Newmarket, Suffolk CB8 7BT.
BRIC aims to be a truly representative voice of its members, from all sides of its industry, to create a better understanding between them, the public and the Government. Finding a normal job through BRIC is unlikely but enquiries into a specific abnormal one may be an idea.

The British Equestrian Federation
National Equestrian Centre, Stoneleigh, Warwickshire.
A recently formed body to help promote better policies and professional involvement in everything to do with British horses and sport.

Organisations in the indutry

The British Equine Veterinary Association
Park Lodge, Bells Yew Green Road, Frant, East Sussex TN3 9EB.
The veterinary surgeons with horse practices formed this branch of the British Veterinary Association to exchange information and ideas on the treatment of horses. Occasionally the secretary knows of a vacancy for a trained veterinary nurse.

National Master Farriers and Blacksmiths Association
674 Lofthouse Lane, Wakefield, Yorkshire.

Farriers Registration Council
4 Royal College Street, London NW1.

Council for Small Industries in Rural Areas (for England)
141 Castle Street, Salisbury, Wiltshire.

Scottish Development Agency (for Scotland)
Small Business Division, 102 Telford Road, Edinburgh EH4 2NP

Welsh Development Agency (for Wales)
Small Business Unit, Treforest Industrial Estate, Pontypridd, Glamorgan CF37 5UT.

The five addresses above all deal with applications for farriery and apprenticeships. Their apprenticeship schemes start at sixteen years so you should get the details before you leave school.

Council for Small Industries in Rural Areas
PO Box 717, 35 Camp Road, Wimbledon, London SW1D 4UP.
This Council is the headquarters of the Government department (Ministry of the Environment), given the task of bringing work and business back to the rural areas for the farrier, saddler and wheel-wright or coachbuilder.

The Jockey Club
42 Portman Square, London W1H 0AP.
This Club controls and licenses the officials and professional members of racing in Britain, and also keeps a record and registration of the employees in the stables.

The stewards take an active part in racing and several boys have found jobs through writing or enquiring at the office.

The British Horse Society
British Equestrian Centre, Kenilworth, Warwickshire CV8 2LR.
The British Horse Society relies on subscriptions to finance its many functions. It is primarily a body organised and elected to set standards and unite the breeders, riders, owners, supporters and various societies for the advancement and benefit of the British horse.

There is a wide variety of services you can get from their enquiries office, which you can telephone Coventry (STD 0203) 52241 and there are ample lines, this is preferred to letters.

Do not ask about jobs as they are not an employment agency, neither do they advise on racing and thoroughbred breeding, although members often are concerned in both. Membership or associate membership is needed to make use of the services.

The National Pony Society
7 Crosse Pillory Lane, Alton, Hampshire.
The society was formed to champion all the native pony breeds. Since then its aims and objectives have widened to include a Junior Judges scheme and several other diploma courses in breaking, breeding, pony management. These are at members establishments and it is difficult to get grants to attend them if you cannot afford the fees.

The Hunters Improvement and Light Horse Breeders Society
or the new name which may be used if agreed
The National Light Horse Breeding Society
8 Market Square, Westerham, Kent.
The revised name has much to do with the new policy of the society. The membership is mainly of people interested in breeding a good type of riding horse. In the past the most popular type was the hunter, now horse trials, team chasing, show-jumpers and utility horses far outnumber the hunting needs and require more athletic and versatile horses.

Organisations in the indutry

The Thoroughbred Breeders Association
168 High Street, Newmarket, Suffolk.
While the main object of the TBA is to encourage producing and improving the thoroughbred horse, its administration does much to help educate and promote good relationships between breeders and their staff. Because of this liaison they often hear of future probably vacancies. This service depends on the goodwill of the secretary and his workload. Therefore, if you do write make the reply easy for him and enclose a stamped addressed envelope.

The Stablelads Association
This association was formed to negotiate a minimum wage for racing staff. Now its activities embrace all the conditions of employment in the Racing Stables. Contact is usually through the Head Lad or a member in the stable. The Secretary, T Delaney, The Granary, Halcomb Stud, Chastleton, Moreton in the Marsh, Gloucestershire. He makes periodical visits to the training centres and can be contacted there or by letter.

National Association of Grooms
PO Box 7, Tetbury, Gloucestershire GL8 8YW.
NAG as the founder members call this non-militant association, tries to improve working conditions and wages for its members in the private stables. Because of the difficulties in establishing these standards, they advise employers and employees on contracts of employment and training to enable them to work in harmony.

Their ideal would be a training and craft structure similar to agriculture. To start the schemes they publish very good pamphlets on apprenticeship, employing and being employed, together with an 'employment contract' for use of members at a cost which only covers printing and postage.

Annual membership of NAG is currently £4 which is excellent value as it enables you to obtain professional advice if you are entering work with horses without any personal contacts in the industry. The register of employment vacancies is a bonus available to members at monthly intervals for another £1.

114

Index

Index